الاستنباط من البحر العميق

AL- ISTINBĀTU MIN AL BAHRI AL A'MÌQ

DROPS FROM THE DEEP OCEAN

REFLECTIONS ON THE QUR'AN

Collective Efforts, Conflicts, and Disputes

with a focus on

► Contemporary Renderings
► Psychological Explorations
► Western Discourses
► Lexical Analysis

VOLUME 8

Dr. M. Yunus Kumek

Address to the Islamic Religious Scholars & Philosophers

Cover Photo by Y. Kumek, Alexandria, Egypt, January 12, 2019.

Medina Houseᶜ
publishing

www.medinahouse.org
170 Manhattan Ave, Po. Box 63
New York 14215
contact@medinahouse.org

Copyright © 2021 by Medina Houseᶜ Publishing

ISBN 978-1-950979-50-9

Published in the United States of America.

TABLE OF CONTENTS

VOLUME 8

بِسْمِ اللهِ الرَّحْمَنِ الرَّحِيمِ[1]

الْحَمْدُ للهِ رَبِّ الْعَالَمِينَ[2]

اللَّهُمَّ صَلِّ عَلَى سَيِّدِنَا وَ حَبِيبِنَا وَ مَوْلَانَا مُحَمَّدٍ[3]

Preface

Harmony of the Qurān

One should know that the verses of the Qurān, the phrases in these verses, the totality of these phrases, the words in these phrases, and even the letters as established with the rules of recitation (tajwid) are similar to the parts of a clock or a watch as depicted below:

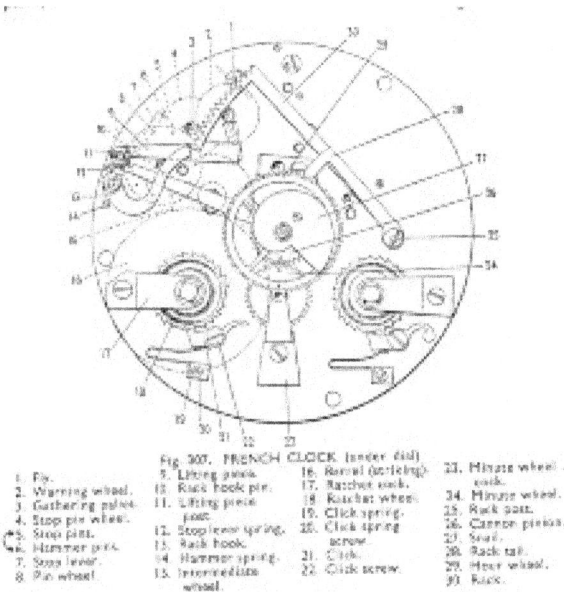

Fig. 307. FRENCH CLOCK (under dial)

1. Fly.	9. Lifting piece.	16. Rental (striking).	23. Minute wheel cock.
2. Warning wheel.	10. Rack hook pin.	17. Ratchet cock.	24. Minute wheel.
3. Gathering pallet.	11. Lifting piece post.	18. Ratchet wheel.	25. Rack post.
4. Stop pin wheel.		19. Click spring.	26. Cannon pinion.
5. Stop pin.	12. Stop lever spring.	20. Click spring screw.	27. Stud.
6. Hammer pin.	13. Rack hook.		28. Rack tail.
7. Stop lever.	14. Hammer spring.	21. Click.	29. Hour wheel.
8. Pin wheel.	15. Intermediate wheel.	22. Click screw.	30. Rack.

---

1. In the name of Allah, the Entirely Merciful, the Especially Merciful.
2. [All] praise is [due] to Allah, Lord of the worlds.
3. O Allah, bless our master, our beloved, and Mawlana Muhammed (PBUH).

© *pixabay*

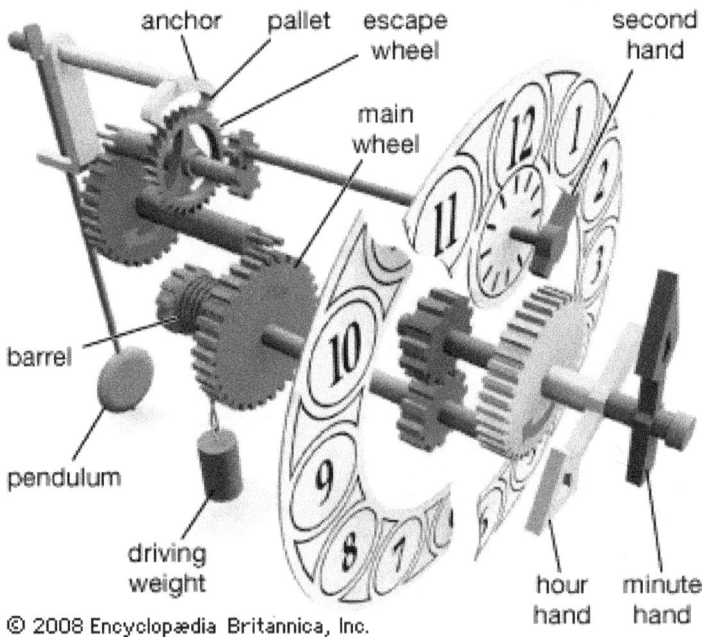

anchor   pallet   escape wheel   second hand

main wheel

barrel

pendulum

driving weight

hour hand   minute hand

© 2008 Encyclopædia Britannica, Inc.

There are different wheels as mentioned in the above diagram. These are the escape wheel, and the main wheel. There are different parts such as pendulum, anchor, pallet, driving weight, hour hand, and minute hand. One helps another. One follows another.

Similarly, the letters of the Qurān help the other letters. The words help other words. The phrases help other phrases. The ayahs help other ayahs. They all support and follow each other. To emphasize this reality, one can remember the constant repetition of the ayahs in the Qurān such as[4]

الْحَمْدُ لِلَّهِ الَّذِي أَنزَلَ عَلَى عَبْدِهِ الْكِتَابَ وَلَمْ يَجْعَل لَّهُ عِوَجَا {الكهف/1}

Harmonizing the Science & Religion

As one review the ayahs of the Qurān, there are the explicit and implicit indications of scientific realities, discoveries, inventions, and different scientific openings for humans. At the same time, within these scientific discussions, one can realize the embedded meanings of Uluhiyyah and Rububiyyah of Allah ﷻ leading to the natural ubudiyyah of Allah ﷻ with love, experience and mental and spiritual agreement, satisfaction and harmony.

In this regard, one can review the ayahs such as[5] يَوْمَ نَطْوِي السَّمَاء كَطَيِّ السِّجِلِّ لِلْكُتُبِ كَمَا بَدَأْنَا أَوَّلَ خَلْقٍ نُّعِيدُهُ وَعْدًا عَلَيْنَا إِنَّا كُنَّا فَاعِلِينَ {الأنبياء/104}. In this ayah, there are some realities that are mentioned with the cosmos and different universes that today's physics and math can be bewildered in their discussions of different abstract dimensions and planes. As a former physicist, I think, these ayahs are critical to give different fields an inductive, top-down openings and inspirations for scientific discoveries as a Mercy, Grace, and Fadl from Allah ﷻ.

One can realize in this perspective that there is the true scholarship harmonizing religion and science. Science and religion do not conflict but serve to the same purpose of La ilaha illa Allah. In this sense, if science is a deductive learning through experimentation, trial and error, then the true religion Islām is the inductive learning through the Qurān and hadith. Both harmonize and triangulate to the same result in a true scholarship. In this regard, a scholar can have the highest level of imān with certainty when witnessing the Divine teachings affirmed and

---

4. [All] praise is [due] to Allah, who has sent down upon His Servant the Book and has not made therein any deviance.
5. The Day when We will fold the heaven like the folding of a [written] sheet for the records. As We began the first creation, We will repeat it. [That is] a promise binding upon Us. Indeed, We will do it.

confirmed with personal expertise approaches of humans in different scientific disciplines.

The reality of these scholars is mentioned in the Qurān as إِنَّمَا يَخْشَى وَمِنَ النَّاسِ وَالدَّوَابِّ وَالْأَنْعَامِ مُخْتَلِفٌ أَلْوَانُهُ كَذَلِكَ in the ayah[6] اللَّهَ مِنْ عِبَادِهِ الْعُلَمَاء إِنَّمَا يَخْشَى اللَّهَ مِنْ عِبَادِهِ الْعُلَمَاء إِنَّ اللَّهَ عَزِيزٌ غَفُورٌ {فاطر/28}. In this regard, one can realize the highest level of the humans are the real scholars in the purpose of creation. Because, in the above ayah, there is a selection of إِنَّمَا يَخْشَى اللَّهَ مِنْ عِبَادِهِ الْعُلَمَاء among other categories of creation as وَمِنَ النَّاسِ وَالدَّوَابِّ وَالْأَنْعَامِ مُخْتَلِفٌ أَلْوَانُهُ

When we review the Quranic content, the content of the Qurān does not only include natural sciences. The Qurān also includes the information about social sciences such as history, psychology, anthropology, economy, and other fields.

One can review the content of the Qurān with the field of for example, history. There are a lot of historical information that was not able to be known or accessible until recent times with modern times of excavations with archaeology and carbon dating. For example, the information presented in the Qurān about the people of Ād, Sāmud and the people of Nûh (عليه السلام). The findings confirm these historical data [1]. At the same time, the Qurān has given information for the future renderings such as mentioned in Sûrah Rum. The news of the Qurān about the future events were constantly confirmed and witnessed by all humanity.

The Qurān also includes a lot of content with humanities in the fields of philosophy (logic)-kalām, communication, language, arts, and music, especially through the vocal recitations of the Qurān and Divine words, dhikr. One should remember that definition of the music is not only instrumental sounds, but it is also defined melodious and harmonious sounds through vocals. Music in one pespective is defined as vocal or instrumental sounds (or both) combined in such a way as to produce beauty of form, harmony, and expression of emotion [2].

The Qurān depicts echoing renderings of the nature, and human interactions of the nature through the expression of sound generation.

---

6. And among people and moving creatures and grazing livestock are various colors similarly. Only those fear Allah, from among His servants, who have knowledge. Indeed, Allah is Exalted in Might and Forgiving.

The Unique Authority

When we analyze the ayahs of the Qurãn, there is a unique authority that is explicitly and clearly different than the human authority. This Authority is the Authority of Allah ﷻ as the Creator, the One, Unique, Sustainer and Maintainer of the all the creation, humans and universes. In this sense, one can clearly see, feel, and understand this uniqueness beyond the human realities, SubhanAllah!

For example, we can just take few ayahs and analyze them as[7]

يَوْمَ نَطْوِي السَّمَاءَ كَطَيِّ السِّجِلِّ لِلْكُتُبِ كَمَا بَدَأْنَا أَوَّلَ خَلْقٍ نُعِيدُهُ وَعْدًا عَلَيْنَا إِنَّا كُنَّا فَاعِلِينَ {الأنبياء/104}

أَفَغَيْرَ دِينِ اللَّهِ يَبْغُونَ وَلَهُ أَسْلَمَ مَن فِي السَّمَاوَاتِ وَالأَرْضِ طَوْعًا وَكَرْهًا وَإِلَيْهِ يُرْجَعُونَ {آل عمران/83}[8]

وَلِلَّهِ يَسْجُدُ مَن فِي السَّمَاوَاتِ وَالأَرْضِ طَوْعًا وَكَرْهًا وَظِلاَلُهُم بِالْغُدُوِّ وَالآصَالِ {الرعد/15}[9]

ثُمَّ اسْتَوَى إِلَى السَّمَاءِ وَهِيَ دُخَانٌ فَقَالَ لَهَا وَلِلْأَرْضِ اِئْتِيَا طَوْعًا أَوْ كَرْهًا قَالَتَا أَتَيْنَا طَائِعِينَ {فصلت/11}[10]

وَلَقَدْ خَلَقْنَا الْإِنسَانَ وَنَعْلَمُ مَا تُوَسْوِسُ بِهِ نَفْسُهُ وَنَحْنُ أَقْرَبُ إِلَيْهِ مِنْ حَبْلِ الْوَرِيدِ {ق/16}[11]

If we analyze the above ayahs, if we for example take an ayah such as[12] وَلِلَّهِ يَسْجُدُ مَن فِي السَّمَاوَاتِ وَالأَرْضِ طَوْعًا وَكَرْهًا وَظِلاَلُهُم بِالْغُدُوِّ وَالآصَالِ {الرعد/15}, if we assume that if a human makes this statement, this person is considered crazy or insane.

---

7. The Day when We will fold the heaven like the folding of a [written] sheet for the records. As We began the first creation, We will repeat it. [That is] a promise binding upon Us. Indeed, We will do it.

8. So is it other than the religion of Allah they desire, while to Him have submitted [all] those within the heavens and earth, willingly or by compulsion, and to Him they will be

9. And to Allah prostrates whoever is within the heavens and the earth, willingly or by compulsion, and their shadows [as well] in the mornings and the afternoons.

10. Then He directed Himself to the heaven while it was smoke and said to it and to the earth, "Come [into being], willingly or by compulsion." They said, "We have come willingly."

11. And We have already created man and know what his soul whispers to him, and We are closer to him than [his] jugular vein

12. And to Allah prostrates whoever is within the heavens and the earth, willingly or by compulsion, and their shadows [as well] in the mornings and the afternoons.

If the highest-level authority of humans such as a king, the president, or Firawn claims or states above content for themselves, as a person who was idolized as the highest level of authority, then he can endanger their position of mind soundness of ruling a country. Because although some of the ignorant and dumb subjects of this highest authority, such as the Firawn, can believe whatever Firawn says. Yet, the people who were in everyday life of Firawn knew the humanness of Firawn with eating, going to bathroom, sleeping etc.

Therefore, Firawn in his close group were not able to claim and argue with his deity argument but he had tried to act as a democratic leader as mentioned[13] قَالَ لِلْمَلَإِ حَوْلَهُ إِنَّ هَذَا لَسَاحِرٌ عَلِيمٌ {الشعراء/34} يُرِيدُ أَن يُخْرِجَكُم مِّنْ أَرْضِكُم بِسِحْرِهِ فَمَاذَا تَأْمُرُونَ {الشعراء/35} قَالُوا أَرْجِهْ وَأَخَاهُ وَابْعَثْ فِي الْمَدَائِنِ حَاشِرِينَ {الشعراء/36}.

With the dumb and ignorant masses, Firawn used a very humiliating argument such as[14]

وَقَالَ فِرْعَوْنُ يَا هَامَانُ ابْنِ لِي صَرْحًا لَّعَلِّي أَبْلُغُ الْأَسْبَابَ {غافر/36} أَسْبَابَ السَّمَاوَاتِ فَأَطَّلِعَ إِلَى إِلَهِ مُوسَى وَإِنِّي لَأَظُنُّهُ كَاذِبًا وَكَذَلِكَ زُيِّنَ لِفِرْعَوْنَ سُوءُ عَمَلِهِ وَصُدَّ عَنِ السَّبِيلِ وَمَا كَيْدُ فِرْعَوْنَ إِلَّا فِي تَبَابٍ {غافر/37}

وَنَادَى فِرْعَوْنُ فِي قَوْمِهِ قَالَ يَا قَوْمِ أَلَيْسَ لِي مُلْكُ مِصْرَ وَهَذِهِ الْأَنْهَارُ تَجْرِي مِن تَحْتِي أَفَلَا تُبْصِرُونَ {الزخرف/51} أَمْ أَنَا خَيْرٌ مِّنْ هَذَا الَّذِي هُوَ مَهِينٌ وَلَا يَكَادُ يُبِينُ {الزخرف/52} فَلَوْلَا أُلْقِيَ عَلَيْهِ أَسْوِرَةٌ مِّن ذَهَبٍ أَوْ جَاء مَعَهُ الْمَلَائِكَةُ مُقْتَرِنِينَ {الزخرف/53}[15] فَاسْتَخَفَّ قَوْمَهُ فَأَطَاعُوهُ إِنَّهُمْ كَانُوا قَوْمًا فَاسِقِينَ {الزخرف/54}

These ignorant ones followed him.

The above discussion underlines that if the above ayahs are mentioned by a human and even the highest authority of the humans

---

13. [Pharaoh] said to the eminent ones around him, "Indeed, this is a learned magician. He wants to drive you out of your land by his magic, so what do you advise?" They said, "Postpone [the matter of] him and his brother and send among the cities gatherers
14. [40:36] And Pharaoh said, "O Haman, construct for me a tower that I might reach the ways— [40:37] The ways into the heavens—so that I may look at the deity of Moses; but indeed, I think he is a liar." And thus was made attractive to Pharaoh the evil of his deed, and he was averted from the [right] way. And the plan of Pharaoh was not except in ruin.
15. [43:51] And Pharaoh called out among his people; he said, "O my people, does not the kingdom of Egypt belong to me, and these rivers flowing beneath me; then do you not see?[43:52] Or am I [not] better than this one who is insignificant and hardly makes himself clear?[43:53] Then why have there not been placed upon him bracelets of gold or come with him the angels in conjunction?"[43:54] So he bluffed his people, and they obeyed him. Indeed, they were [themselves] a people defiantly disobedient [of Allah].

today or historically, they would be considered insane and sent to a hospital for treatment. If they are existing among present authority holders, then they would lose their existing power and authority due to not properly manipulating the masses. Firawn manipulated the masses wisely that he used a double language.

Firawn used an authoritative language for general ignorant masses referred as the weak or dumb ones and humiliated them in their weakness by manipulating them. This is mentioned as فَاسْتَخَفَّ قَوْمَهُ فَأَطَاعُوهُ إِنَّهُمْ كَانُوا قَوْمًا فَاسِقِينَ {الزخرف/54}

Some of the general public knew the reality of humanness of Firawn but followed and obeyed Firawn due to fear.

Firawn used a democratic language of humanness to his close circle because his close circle knew Firawn that he was just a limited weak human.

Styles of Confrontation (Munazara)

In effect, in this close circle, there was the case of a high level of authority holder as the believer of Allah ﷻ as referred as mumin min al-I firawan in the Qurān. He was a reasonable and intelligent man who used also a double language for the immediate circle and general masses in order to counter Firawn's argument.

For the inner and higher circle of authority, he used a language of reason and convincement as[16] وَقَالَ رَجُلٌ مُّؤْمِنٌ مِّنْ آلِ فِرْعَوْنَ يَكْتُمُ إِيمَانَهُ أَتَقْتُلُونَ رَجُلًا أَن يَقُولَ رَبِّيَ اللَّهُ وَقَدْ جَاءكُم بِالْبَيِّنَاتِ مِن رَّبِّكُمْ وَإِن يَكُ كَاذِبًا فَعَلَيْهِ كَذِبُهُ وَإِن يَكُ صَادِقًا يُصِبْكُم بَعْضُ الَّذِي يَعِدُكُمْ إِنَّ اللَّهَ لَا يَهْدِي مَنْ هُوَ مُسْرِفٌ كَذَّابٌ {غافر/28} يَا قَوْمِ لَكُمُ الْمُلْكُ الْيَوْمَ ظَاهِرِينَ فِي الْأَرْضِ فَمَن يَنصُرُنَا مِن بَأْسِ اللَّهِ إِن جَاءنَا قَالَ فِرْعَوْنُ مَا أُرِيكُمْ إِلَّا مَا أَرَى وَمَا أَهْدِيكُمْ إِلَّا سَبِيلَ الرَّشَادِ {غافر/29}

In the inner circle of authority, Fir'awn understood the confrontation and took this challenge of this believer on himself and try to respond and counter in a very calm and convincing way as mentioned قَالَ فِرْعَوْنُ

---

16. And a believing man from the family of Pharaoh who concealed his faith said, "Do you kill a man [merely] because he says, 'My Lord is Allah' while he has brought you clear proofs from your Lord? And if he should be lying, then upon him is [the consequence of] his lie; but if he should be truthful, there will strike you some of what he promises you. Indeed, Allah does not guide one who is a transgressor and a liar. O my people, sovereignty is yours today, [your being] dominant in the land. But who would protect us from the punishment of Allah if it came to us?" Pharaoh said, "I do not show you except what I see, and I do not guide you except to the way of right conduct."

مَا أُرِيكُمْ إِلَّا مَا أَرَى وَمَا أَهْدِيكُمْ إِلَّا سَبِيلَ الرَّشَادِ {غافر/29}. Because, at this level of inner circle, everyone can be more or less at the same level although Firawn can be the figure for outsiders to be the leader or the deity. In the countering of Firawn in the inner circle, we don't know if Firawn was really sincere or still manipulating in his statement as قَالَ فِرْعَوْنُ مَا أُرِيكُمْ إِلَّا مَا أَرَى وَمَا أَهْدِيكُمْ إِلَّا سَبِيلَ الرَّشَادِ {غافر/29}.

Then, Mumin al-Firawn used a language for general masses for that he, Mumin al-Firawn should be followed for guidance compared to the cases of threating authority of Firawn instilling fear to his subjects under his ruling. These two similar but also different cases are mentioned for Mumin al-Firawn and Firawn respectively as:[17]

وَقَالَ الَّذِي آمَنَ يَا قَوْمِ اتَّبِعُونِ أَهْدِكُمْ سَبِيلَ الرَّشَادِ {غافر/38}

قَالَ آمَنتُمْ لَهُ قَبْلَ أَنْ آذَنَ لَكُمْ إِنَّهُ لَكَبِيرُكُمُ الَّذِي عَلَّمَكُمُ السِّحْرَ فَلَسَوْفَ تَعْلَمُونَ لَأُقَطِّعَنَّ أَيْدِيَكُمْ وَأَرْجُلَكُم مِّنْ خِلَافٍ وَلَأُصَلِّبَنَّكُمْ أَجْمَعِينَ {الشعراء/49}[18]

In other words, Mumin al-Firawn used exactly the same method of Firawn to nullify and destroy Firawn's argument. Therefore, sometimes in balagah or in the fields of debate (munazara), a party can use exactly the same term or expression to refute the claim of the other party. This can be one of the strongest way of nullifying a proposed argument.

This style can be also vivid in the Qurān. For example,[19] إِنَّ الله لَا يَسْتَحْيِي أَن يَضْرِبَ مَثَلاً مَّا بَعُوضَةً فَمَا فَوْقَهَا فَأَمَّا الَّذِينَ آمَنُواْ فَيَعْلَمُونَ أَنَّهُ الْحَقُّ مِن رَّبِّهِمْ وَأَمَّا الَّذِينَ كَفَرُواْ فَيَقُولُونَ مَاذَا أَرَادَ اللَّهُ بِهَذَا مَثَلاً يُضِلُّ بِهِ كَثِيراً وَيَهْدِي بِهِ كَثِيراً وَمَا يُضِلُّ بِهِ إِلاَّ الْفَاسِقِينَ {البقرة/26}. The people of Makkah try to make a case against the Qurān by using the word يَسْتَحْيِي for Allah ﷻ, Astagfirullah. The Qurān uses their own argument against them to counter and refute their claim with the same word as إِنَّ اللهَ لاَ يَسْتَحْيِي أَن يَضْرِبَ مَثَلاً مَّا بَعُوضَةً فَمَا يَسْتَحْيِي in فَوْقَهَا.

SubhanAllah!

---

17. And he who believed said, "O my people, follow me, I will guide you to the way of right conduct.

18. [Pharaoh] said, "You believed Moses before I gave you permission. Indeed, he is your leader who has taught you magic, but you are going to know. I will surely cut off your hands and your feet on opposite sides, and I will surely crucify you all."

19. Indeed, Allah is not timid to present an example—that of a mosquito or what is smaller than it. And those who have believed know that it is the truth from their Lord. But as for those who disbelieve, they say, "What did Allah intend by this as an example?" He misleads many thereby and guides many thereby. And He misleads not except the defiantly disobedient,

The Reality of the Real and Pseudo Authority & Understanding the Hadith Qudsi about Kibriya

It is very important to realize that when humans try to act in an absolute authority as mentioned قَالَ آمَنتُمْ لَهُ قَبْلَ أَنْ آذَنَ لَكُمْ إِنَّهُ لَكَبِيرُكُمُ الَّذِي عَلَّمَكُمُ السِّحْرَ ,فَلَسَوْفَ تَعْلَمُونَ لَأُقَطِّعَنَّ أَيْدِيَكُمْ وَأَرْجُلَكُم مِّنْ خِلَافٍ وَلَأُصَلِّبَنَّكُمْ أَجْمَعِينَ {الشعراء/49} this unbefitting and unsuitable act really looks funny and inappropriate on limited weak and in need humans and all creation.

The rebellion attitudes and trends today and in the past towards authority in parent-children relations, husband-wife relations, and in all authority related relations in a society can stem due to these unfitting cases of humans trying to disguise the Kibriya and A'zamah of Allah ﷻ. Yet, Allah ﷻ mentions the Kibriyah and A'zamah of Allah ﷻ only belongs to Allah ﷻ and whoever takes to claim something with this, then they will be humiliated [5] [4] [3].

May Allah ﷻ protect us, Amìn.

Contemporaneity of the Qurān

One of the very interesting and remarkable features of the Qurān is that the Qurān is always contemporary of all the times. People and ideas die, disappear and become old and unused but the Qurān is always contemporary of the time of the century, era, year, month or the minute.

Again, this is one of the miracles of the Qurān as being from Rabbul Alamìn, al-Bakì, al-Hayy and al-Qayyûm.

In other words, the content and teachings of the Qurān do not get old but they are always fresh. It is as if they are showing a goal for humanity to reach with its contemporaneity, and harmony with the understandings of time and space.

Solutions for the Social Problems from the Qurānic Perspective

One of the remarkable features of the Qurān is that the Qurān gives lessons, teachings and principles about the communal life. One of the things that we constantly deal with is the social problems. These social, group, or communal problems can be in the family, at work, or in the society. Society, community, or group are all terms to indicate the cases as soon as with interact with another individual.

One should realize that each human is similar to a universe in its complexity [6]. If one can consider a human interacting with another human, then one can consider a complex universe is interacting with another complex universe. If one considers families or family dynamics, or societies or the global world that we are living, then one can now consider billion complex universes are interacting other billion universes.

In these interactions if there are not certain principles, and guidelines, a peaceful life can become chaotic, miserable and painful as mentioned[20] ظَهَرَ الْفَسَادُ فِي الْبَرِّ وَالْبَحْرِ بِمَا كَسَبَتْ أَيْدِي النَّاسِ لِيُذِيقَهُم بَعْضَ الَّذِي عَمِلُوا لَعَلَّهُمْ يَرْجِعُونَ {الروم/41}.

Therefore, policies, laws and constitutions are present to explain these principles and enforce them.

In this sense, it is very critical to focus the humanly made principles and compare them Divinely instructed principles.

Today, due to the negative attitudes toward religion, humanly principles override Divinely principles in policy making. Then, we try to find solutions to our problems that we introduce in our policies.

When one analyzes the Quranic principles of the social life, then one can deduce meanings to minimize the social problems and social conflicts.

In the complex billion interaction of universes, principles, guidelines, policies or constitutions are only some simple means to establish order and structure in these humanly interactions. Yet, it is very difficult to really establish order and structure in these interactions. Humanly order and structures can be helpful but, yet it will be always superficial not addressing the real problem if Divinely principles are not considered.

Therefore, since the angels knew this reality, they mentioned and objected the reality of the creation of humans as[21] وَإِذْ قَالَ رَبُّكَ لِلْمَلَائِكَةِ إِنِّي

---

20. Corruption has appeared throughout the land and sea by [reason of] what the hands of people have earned so He may let them taste part of [the consequence of] what they have done that perhaps they will return [to righteousness].
21. And [mention, O Muhammad], when your Lord said to the angels, "Indeed, I will make upon the earth a successive authority." They said, "Will You place upon it one who causes corruption therein and sheds blood, while we declare Your praise and sanctify You?" Allah said, "Indeed, I know that which you do not know."

جَاعِلٌ فِي الأَرْضِ خَلِيفَةً قَالُواْ أَتَجْعَلُ فِيهَا مَن يُفْسِدُ فِيهَا وَيَسْفِكُ الدِّمَاء وَنَحْنُ نُسَبِّحُ بِحَمْدِكَ وَنُقَدِّسُ لَكَ قَالَ إِنِّي أَعْلَمُ مَا لاَ تَعْلَمُونَ {البقرة/30}. Because, humans have the tendency to act arrogant and not consider Divinely Principles through scriptures or prophets, they think that they are sufficient with secular mind related applications.

Yet, one of the missing parts of the major fundamental part in humanly established guidelines and divine guidelines is the law enforcement perspectives. In humanly guidelines, there are consequences in this life. In Divinely guidelines, there are consequences both in this life and afterlife. A religious person can think twice before breaking a law because even if the humanly law enforcement officer may not catch this person's planned offense, Allah ﷻ knows and monitors this person in all his internal emotional, intentional and external engagements.

In this sense, the Qurān establishes a self-accountability procedure, guidelines and principles for each human being or in each complex universe before they interact with others.

The fields of tasawwuf leading to raise humans to move beyond self-interest-based motivations into the altruistic motivations is itself a main and core separate science and discipline in the teachings of the Qurān and sunnah of Rasulullah ﷺ.

Interreacting with others or other universes should be in line with the principle of the self-universe teachings of the tasawwuf outlined from the Qurān and sunnah of Rasulullah ﷺ.

This, then entail altruistic behaviors of consideration, empathy, accountability in front of the One Who is aware of everything.

The Field of Psychology in the Qurān

The Arabic term for psychology is ilmul-nafs. The definition of psychology is in Oxford dictionary "the scientific study of the human mind and its functions, especially those affecting behavior in a given context," [2].

When review the term "ilmul-nafs" as translated from Arabic for psychology, nafs does not necessarily mean mind. Mind has a separate term as aqil. The definition of nafs, sometimes translated as self or ego has complicated parameters. In this sense, mind or aqil is one of the parameters affecting the nafs.

Although there are these fundamental differences between Islamic and Western terminologies for the corresponding approaches of disciplines, one can review the Quranic content with the current defined notions of Western discipline of psychology focusing on behavior, emotions and decision making in the self and collective selves forming the groups.

In this regard, one can realize that there is the individual psychology, family psychology, social psychology , the psychologies of hope and fear and other perspectives of psychology engaging both common readers and experts with the techniques of psychoanalysis.

VOLUME 8

Sûrah 2 – al-Baqara

[25]

وَبَشِّرِ الَّذِينَ آمَنُواْ وَعَمِلُواْ الصَّالِحَاتِ أَنَّ لَهُمْ جَنَّاتٍ تَجْرِي مِن تَحْتِهَا الأَنْهَارُ كُلَّمَا رُزِقُواْ مِنْهَا مِن ثَمَرَةٍ رِّزْقاً قَالُواْ هَذَا الَّذِي رُزِقْنَا مِن قَبْلُ وَأُتُواْ بِهِ مُتَشَابِهاً وَلَهُمْ فِيهَا أَزْوَاجٌ مُّطَهَّرَةٌ وَهُمْ فِيهَا خَالِدُونَ {البقرة/25}[22]

If we review the ayahs of the Qurān in Sûrah Baqarah until this ayah, a very interesting notion reveals about the style of the Qurān. Also, another interesting notion reveals about the high position of Rasulullah ﷺ in this communication style, SubhanAllah!

When we analyze different styles of the Qurān in presenting the content, sometimes Allah ﷻ directly mentions the content of the topic without any dialogue or discourse involving others. For example,[23] ذَلِكَ الْكِتَابُ لاَ رَيْبَ فِيهِ هُدًى لِّلْمُتَّقِينَ {البقرة/2}.

In some cases, there is a conversation or dialogue reported as[24] وَإِذَا قِيلَ لَهُمْ آمِنُواْ كَمَا آمَنَ النَّاسُ قَالُواْ أَنُؤْمِنُ كَمَا آمَنَ السُّفَهَاء أَلا إِنَّهُمْ هُمُ السُّفَهَاءُ وَلَكِن لاَّ يَعْلَمُونَ {البقرة/13}

Sometimes, there is address of addressee with the notions of iltifāt, changing the pronoun from mutakallim to ghayib, second to third pronoun. For example,[25] فَإِن لَّمْ تَفْعَلُواْ وَلَن تَفْعَلُواْ فَاتَّقُواْ النَّارَ الَّتِي وَقُودُهَا النَّاسُ وَالْحِجَارَةُ أُعِدَّتْ لِلْكَافِرِينَ {البقرة/24}

Sometimes, there is a direct address of Rasulullah ﷺ as the messenger and prophet of Allah ﷻ communicating and informing the content of the Qurān to others. For example, a very common example is with the repeated word of قُلْ as in for example[26] قُلْ هُوَ اللَّهُ أَحَدٌ {الإخلاص/1}.

---

22. And give good tidings to those who believe and do righteous deeds that they will have gardens [in Paradise] beneath which rivers flow. Whenever they are provided with a provision of fruit therefrom, they will say, "This is what we were provided with before." And it is given to them in likeness. And they will have therein purified spouses, and they will abide therein eternally.
23. This is the Book about which there is no doubt, a guidance for those conscious of Allah -
24. And when it is said to them, "Believe as the people have believed," they say, "Should we believe as the foolish have believed?" Unquestionably, it is they who are the foolish, but they know [it] not.
25. But if you do not—and you will never be able to—then fear the Fire, whose fuel is men and stones, prepared for the disbelievers.
26. Say, "He is Allah, [who is] One,

In all of these above cases and others, there is the balāgah, ijāz and very intrinsic, deep, convoluted, amazing, astonishing, miraculous and mind-blowing perspectives of the Qurān as the original and authentic scripture from Allah ﷻ.

One of these mind-blowing perspectives is that one of the first addressee of Rasulullah ﷺ in an explicit way is with this ayah as[27] وَبَشِّرِ الَّذِينَ آمَنُواْ وَعَمِلُواْ الصَّالِحَاتِ أَنَّ لَهُمْ جَنَّاتٍ تَجْرِي مِن تَحْتِهَا الأَنْهَارُ كُلَّمَا رُزِقُواْ مِنْهَا مِن ثَمَرَةٍ رِّزْقاً قَالُواْ هَذَا الَّذِي رُزِقْنَا مِن قَبْلُ وَأُتُواْ بِهِ مُتَشَابِهاً وَلَهُمْ فِيهَا أَزْوَاجٌ مُطَهَّرَةٌ وَهُمْ فِيهَا خَالِدُونَ {البقرة/25}.

The first word of this explicit addressing style is وَبَشِّر. Rasulullah ﷺ is al-Bashìr. His first attribute in the Qurān is presented as al-Bashìr. He ﷺ is also al-Nazìr. Yet, the first style of explicit communication with Rasulullah ﷺ emphasizes his perspective of mercy, Rahmah and giving the glad tidings. This is mentioned in[28] وَمَا أَرْسَلْنَاكَ إِلَّا رَحْمَةً لِّلْعَالَمِينَ {الأنبياء/107}.

Active Imān and Definition of Amalu-Sālih

The expression الَّذِينَ آمَنُواْ وَعَمِلُواْ الصَّالِحَاتِ focuses on the qualities of a believer. In this regard, الَّذِينَ آمَنُواْ وَعَمِلُواْ الصَّالِحَاتِ can indicate an active imān. The expression عَمِلُواْ الصَّالِحَاتِ can be defined as good actions that please Allah ﷻ. Any good-seeming action that does not please Allah ﷻ is not عَمِلُواْ الصَّالِحَاتِ. Therefore, even though people may applaud the person for humanly and socially constructed good or virtuous, if Allah ﷻ is not pleased with it as part of the عَمِلُواْ الصَّالِحَاتِ, then that action does not have really any real value. This can be similar to a money game. There are thousands or millions of dollars that can have a value in this money game. If this child wants to buy something with this fake money in real life, the people will laugh at him.

Similarly, amalu-sālih, good or virtuous seeming engagements that does not have any value by Allah ﷻ is not عَمِلُواْ الصَّالِحَاتِ. In the game of the world, people may value it but in reality, they don't have any value. May Allah ﷻ make us involve with عَمِلُواْ الصَّالِحَاتِ, Amìn.

---

27. And give good tidings to those who believe and do righteous deeds that they will have gardens [in Paradise] beneath which rivers flow. Whenever they are provided with a provision of fruit therefrom, they will say, "This is what we were provided with before." And it is given to them in likeness. And they will have therein purified spouses, and they will abide therein eternally.

28. And We have not sent you, [O Muhammad], except as a mercy to the worlds.

The Pain of the Knowledge of Temporality for Humans

When we analyze the expression[29] {البقرة/25} وَهُمْ فِيهَا خَالِدُونَ, one can consider this expression from the reality of its opposite present today in this life for humans.

One of the intrinsic deteriorating and destroying feelings for humans is the knowledge of temporality of the pleasures, friendships, and engagements.

If a person knows the pleasures that he or she is in and will eventually end, then this knowledge actually adds pain and decrease the pleasure of this engagement.

If a person enjoys the life with different means and if he constantly realizes that one day he or she is going to die, then then this knowledge actually adds pain and decrease the pleasure of this engagement.

Then, the pain of temporality really ruins the pleasures of engagements in this world.

Therefore, Allah ﷻ emphasizes in this ayah with وَهُمْ فِيهَا خَالِدُونَ {البقرة/25} that there will not be the pain of temporality. The person will not be worried about this ending and temporal feature of this pleasure. Actually, in reality, permanency knowledge of this reality as mentioned with وَهُمْ فِيهَا خَالِدُونَ {البقرة/25} actually will add more enjoyment and increase the pleasure of the engagements in the afterlife.

Some of the scholars assert that this is one of the differences between humans and animals. Humans' knowledge of temporality in this life adding pain and decreasing the worldly pleasures is different than animals. Animals do not have this knowledge. Therefore, they don't have pain and decrease of pleasure compared to humans. Humans have mind and aqil. They think about the past, present and future. One of the classical definitions of humans in their comparison with humans is that humans are beings/animals with aqil and mind compared to animals. Although this definition can have some points to explain, yet full acceptance of this definition can be problematic, Allahu A'lam.

---

29. And give good tidings to those who believe and do righteous deeds that they will have gardens [in Paradise] beneath which rivers flow. Whenever they are provided with a provision of fruit therefrom, they will say, "This is what we were provided with before." And it is given to them in likeness. And they will have therein purified spouses, and they will abide therein eternally.

[26]

إِنَّ اللَّهَ لاَ يَسْتَحْيِي أَن يَضْرِبَ مَثَلاً مَّا بَعُوضَةً فَمَا فَوْقَهَا فَأَمَّا الَّذِينَ آمَنُواْ فَيَعْلَمُونَ أَنَّهُ الْحَقُّ مِن رَّبِّهِمْ وَأَمَّا الَّذِينَ كَفَرُواْ فَيَقُولُونَ مَاذَا أَرَادَ اللَّهُ بِهَذَا مَثَلاً يُضِلُّ بِهِ كَثِيراً وَيَهْدِي بِهِ كَثِيراً وَمَا يُضِلُّ بِهِ إِلاَّ الْفَاسِقِينَ {البقرة/26}[30]

الَّذِينَ يَنقُضُونَ عَهْدَ اللَّهِ مِن بَعْدِ مِيثَاقِهِ وَيَقْطَعُونَ مَا أَمَرَ اللَّهُ بِهِ أَن يُوصَلَ وَيُفْسِدُونَ فِي الأَرْضِ أُولَئِكَ هُمُ الْخَاسِرُونَ {البقرة/27}[31]

When we analyze the words in the above ayahs, the presence of إِنَّ can indicate the existence of doubts and skepticism. Therefore, there is a ta'kid of an oath to show the opposite in order to remove the doubts.

It is important to give examples to clarify the points. The usage of أَن يَضْرِبَ can indicate the authentication through stamping or benchmarking for the truth and strength of the concept presented in the explanation. In this case, giving examples can be similar to this stamping and authentication when there is an explanation.

When we analyze the expression إِنَّ اللَّهَ لاَ يَسْتَحْيِي, one can realize that the word يَسْتَحْيِي is used for Allah ﷻ. This can be due to the response of the ahlu-kitāb-Yahūd about this word يَسْتَحْيِي to criticize the Qurān that the Qurān mentioned some of the animals such as a fly or a spider [7]. Sometimes in balagah and the field of debate, a party can use exactly the same term or expression to refute the claim of the other party. This is one of the strongest way of nullifying a proposed argument. In this regard, one should view the usage of يَسْتَحْيِي in relation to Allah ﷻ within this context. Allahu A'lam.

When we analyze the word أَن يَضْرِبَ in the statement إِنَّ اللَّهَ لاَ يَسْتَحْيِي أَن يَضْرِبَ مَثَلاً مَّا بَعُوضَةً, one can realize that يَضْرِب is a verb. This can indicate their objection is not the methodology of giving example but their objection is the specific example of بَعُوضَةً.

When we analyze the expression فَأَمَّا الَّذِينَ آمَنُواْ, the sifah or attribute آمَنُوا is emphasized with the sila form instead of mentioning as mu'minūn.

---

30. Indeed, Allah is not timid to present an example—that of a mosquito or what is smaller than it. And those who have believed know that it is the truth from their Lord. But as for those who disbelieve, they say, "What did Allah intend by this as an example?" He misleads many thereby and guides many thereby. And He misleads not except the defiantly disobedient,
31. Who break the covenant of Allah after contracting it and sever that which Allah has ordered to be joined and cause corruption on earth. It is those who are the losers.

Similarly, the same perspective is valid for the case of kufr with the sila form. Their rejection is due to kufr.

Although there is a lot of balagah and style with the mention of مَّا بَعُوضَةً, yet the emphasis is not on its baligh or stylistic excellence, but the emphasis is that the Qurān and all the content of the Qurān is from Allah ﷻ as the reality and the truth as mentioned أَنَّهُ الْحَقُّ.

In the structure of the sentence يُضِلُّ بِهِ كَثِيراً وَيَهْدِي بِهِ كَثِيراً وَمَا يُضِلُّ بِهِ إِلاَّ الْفَاسِقِينَ, one can ask why the word/verb يُضِلُّ comes before يَهْدِي although in the initial part فَأَمَّا الَّذِينَ آمَنُواْ presented first in order? One of the possibilities is that the preference of يُضِلُّ as the taqdīm can indicate their objection for the given example with an immediate rejection. Especially, the repetition of يُضِلُّ can indicate this emphasis because the main content of their approach is their attitude of kufr towards the ayahs and examples given in the Qurān and all in different parts of the universe.

The Hidden Mystery for Guidance: Attitudes

When one analyses the expression[32] فَأَمَّا الَّذِينَ آمَنُواْ فَيَعْلَمُونَ أَنَّهُ الْحَقُّ مِن رَّبِّهِمْ وَأَمَّا الَّذِينَ كَفَرُواْ فَيَقُولُونَ مَاذَا أَرَادَ اللهُ بِهَذَا مَثَلاً, one can clearly discover the hidden mystery of guidance. That are the attitudes, attitudes, and the attitudes.

A case is presented as[33] أَن يَضْرِبَ مَثَلًا مَّا بَعُوضَةً. Yet, on one side the attitude of imān as[34] فَأَمَّا الَّذِينَ آمَنُواْ فَيَعْلَمُونَ أَنَّهُ الْحَقُّ مِن رَّبِّهِمْ. On the other hand, the attitude of kufr is as[35] وَأَمَّا الَّذِينَ كَفَرُواْ فَيَقُولُونَ مَاذَا أَرَادَ اللهُ بِهَذَا مَثَلاً.

One can realize the symmetry of وَأَمَّا and فَأَمَّا. This is the symmetry and polarity of imān and kufr. This symmetry shows the two opposite attitudes.

One is the root attitude for guidance. A person of imān has the humble, accepting, considerate, caring, soft, lenient, gentle and emphatic attitudes and character. A person of imān avoids fully to break someone's heart. Even though a person of imān can seem harsh externally as mentioned to establish order or structure, but yet this external harshness is only a dress, but it does not exist inside. Even if he acts for a purpose to establish discipline, when he is by himself and with Allah ﷻ in self-

---

32. And those who have believed know that it is the truth from their Lord. But as for those who disbelieve, they say, "What did Allah intend by this as an example?"
33. to present an example - that of a mosquito or what is smaller than it.
34. And those who have believed know that it is the truth from their Lord.
35. But as for those who disbelieve, they say, "What did Allah intend by this as an example?"

accountability, he cries and cries for the possibility of oppressing others with this purposeful external costumery harshness. Next day, if he feels and decides after the self-accountability about crossing the boundaries with the subjects of a lower authority, he or she then apologizes and asks forgiveness from them.

When there is no need to establish order and structure in affairs of justice, he or she can act in such a soft and lenient way that he or she is so gentle, caring, smiling, embracing. He prefers silence over talking in case he may break someone's heart. He looks down on the ground in case he hurts or make someone uncomfortable with his looks. He keeps the constant smile on his face in order to make people feel comfortable, welcoming, and easy. Yet, his inside may be spiritually bleeding in the constant worries of others, for their imān to Allah ﷻ, and also worried about not fully embodying the levels of ihsan with gratitude, thankfulness and appreciation for Allah ﷻ.

All above embodiment is the description of Rasulullah ﷺ. If one wants to see and realize a good example of the person of imān, then that is Rasulullah ﷺ. May Allah ﷻ make us follow his ﷺ footsteps, Amìn.

A person of kufr does not care about others. A person of kufr can break hearts. A person of kufr can act vulgar, rude, and intimidating. A person of kufr acts and embodies selfishness. A person of kufr only motivates him or herself with interest. This interest can be based on money, position, recognition, or fame. With these interests, he or she can imitate to act nice. If there are none of these interests, the real self of the person of kufr reveals itself with vulgar, rude, and oppressive attitudes.

Nifãq or munafiq is the highest level of the person of kufr. A person of nifaq or munafiq acts good similar to a person of imān due to interests.

Kufr as a general term or kãfir is generally used for the person who displays explicitly the characters of the person of kufr.

Munafiq is the person who displays implicitly the characters of the person of kufr.

Munafiq is at a lower than the kãfir. Munafiq even lies and acts about his or her real self. On the other hand, kãfir shows his or her real attitude. Munafiq in that sense is sneaky and dublitious. Kafir is belligerent and aggressive. Both are low, and they can work together on the path of Shaytãn. May Allah ﷻ protect us from having any of the traits of the person of kufr and nifãq, Amìn.

Animals in the Qurān

When we review the animal selection of the Qurān such as بَعُوضَةً,
one can realize really many wisdoms and reasons although the early
non-Muslims did not realize this reality. They did not understand the
universality and contemporality of the Qurān. They just viewed the
Qurān within their regional, educational and time related limitations.

As we observe the animals, and all the items that are presented in
the Qurān, there is always relevance to the person regardless of the time,
region, climate and culture.

In this regard, an ant, a fly, a mosquito, a spider, a bird, a bee, a dog,
a tree, a bush, a sheep, a horse, a cow, the sky, the sun, the moon, the
stars, the sea, the ships, a fish, and others have been always accessible to
the humans in their daily life.

Allah ﷻ has many other billion creations, animals, insects, and other
beings. Yet, one of the hikmah is constant accessibility of the people to
these animals to ponder on them and relate them to Rabbul Alamīn,
Allah ﷻ.

In some cases, this accessibility to them is in such a way that the
person does not really do an effort even to look for them. Even, if the
person is confined in a place such as if he is placed in a prison any other
such place with the existence of these beings, Allah ﷻ gives hope and
reminds to these people about their purpose and meaning who may be
in the states of pessimism and hopelessness.

For example, if a person in prison or in a cell confined and oppressed
can have the utmost tendencies of hopelessness and pessimism if they
don't have the strong imān in Allah ﷻ about purpose and meaning in
life. Even, these pessimisms can put the person in such states that the
person can be in the dark states of hopelessness of kufr and consider
committing suicide with depression.

In these shattered mental states, when a person sees a fly, or an ant,
or a spider in this prison that no one can access, then a person who is in
the states of reflection and critical thinking can be inspired with this tiny
looking animal. Although no one can access, these animals can still have
the access to these places of confinement. They can be an harbinger,
bringing message to them from Rabbul Alamin.

SubhanAllah!

In their existence, they all say that everything has a purpose, meaning and life as maintained by Rabbul Alamin. Then, these small looking creatures, and normally not too much welcomed animals and beings in our normal lives, can become the friends of this hopeless person, inspiring him giving hope, meaning, and purpose in life. Then, this person becomes transformed from the darkness of kufr to the lights and hope of imān with the Fadl, Rahmah of Allah ﷻ as mentioned[36]

اللَّهُ وَلِيُّ الَّذِينَ آمَنُواْ يُخْرِجُهُم مِّنَ الظُّلُمَاتِ إِلَى النُّورِ وَالَّذِينَ كَفَرُواْ أَوْلِيَآؤُهُمُ الطَّاغُوتُ يُخْرِجُونَهُم مِّنَ النُّورِ إِلَى الظُّلُمَاتِ أُوْلَئِكَ أَصْحَابُ النَّارِ هُمْ فِيهَا خَالِدُونَ {البقرة/257}

There can be specific significance of some animals or items that can be especially historically significant and accessible still globally but can be dominant in one region today. These can be camels, date trees or snakes. In this regard, these specific and still accessible may need more focus to ponder. For example, the special creation of camels as mentioned[37] أَفَلَا يَنظُرُونَ إِلَى الْإِبِلِ كَيْفَ خُلِقَتْ {الغاشية/17}.

Purpose of Examples

When we analyze the word مَثَلاً, one can think and consider the general usage of examples in a text, writing and the literature. Some of the usage of giving an example is to make the person feel and experience with emotions something that is explained with logic and reason. Another usage could be the opposite of this. It is to explain something abstract, emotional or experiential with something visible, and concrete logical and rational examples.

Micro & Angstrom and Further Realities

When we review the expression مَّا بَعُوضَةً فَمَا فَوْقَهَا, the phrase مَّا can indicate that the example of بَعُوضَةً is just a regular example. There are things similar to its size or smaller or bigger that can have similar and more complex systems.

---

36. Allah is the ally of those who believe. He brings them out from darknesses into the light. And those who disbelieve—their allies are Taghut. They take them out of the light into darknesses. Those are the companions of the Fire; they will abide eternally therein.
37. Then do they not look at the camels—how they are created?

In this regard, this expression مَّا بَعُوضَةً فَمَا فَوْقَهَا can indicate these complex systems in micro and angstrom levels of small scale relative to the humans.

When we look at any ordinary dictionary [2], for example, one can realize today's terminalized realities with the advancement of size at these small scales of micro. For example,

- ▶ microbiology |ˌmaɪkroʊ.baɪˈɑlədʒi| the branch of science that deals with microorganisms.
- ▶ microorganism |ˌmaɪkroʊˈɔrɡənɪzəm| a microscopic organism, especially a bacterium, virus, or fungus.
- ▶ microbiome |ˌmaɪkroʊˈbaɪoʊm|
- ▶ the combined genetic material of the microorganisms in a particular environment: understanding the microbiome—human, animal, and environmental—is as important as the human genome.
- ▶ microRNA |ˌmaɪkroʊ.ɑrɛnˈeɪ| *Genetics* a cellular RNA fragment that prevents the production of a particular protein by binding to and destroying the messenger RNA that would have produced the protein.
- ▶ microbe |ˈmaɪ.kroʊb| a microorganism, especially a bacterium causing disease or fermentation.
- ▶ the microorganisms in a particular environment (including the body or a part of the body): we depend on a vast army of microbes to stay alive: a microbiome that protects us against germs, breaks down food to release energy, and produces vitamins.
- ▶ microwave
- ▶ an electromagnetic wave with a wavelength in the range 0.001–0.3 m, shorter than that of a normal radio wave but longer than those of infrared radiation. Microwaves are used in radar, in communications, and for heating in microwave ovens and in various industrial processes.
- ▶ microvascular |ˌmaɪkroʊˈvæskjələr| adjective of or relating to the smallest blood vessels.
- ▶ microtubule |ˈmaɪkroʊ.t(j)ubjul| *Biology* a microscopic tubular structure present in numbers in the cytoplasm

of cells, sometimes aggregating to form more complex structures [2].

One can realize how these existing creation of Allah ﷻ can lead humans to emulate and imitate in their endeavors of scientific discoveries and applications. Some of the examples are:

► microcomputer |ˈmaɪkroʊkəmˌpjudər| a small computer that contains a microprocessor as its central processor.

► microcell |ˈmaɪkroʊˌsɛl| a small mobile phone base station connected to the phone network via the Internet, typically used to improve mobile phone reception within a particular area

► microcircuit |ˈmaɪkroʊˌsərkət| a minute electric circuit, especially an integrated circuit.

► microdot |ˈmaɪkrəˌdɑt| a microphotograph, especially of a printed or written document, that is only about 0.04 inch (1 mm) across.• [usu. as modifier] denoting a pattern of very small dots.

► microkernel |ˈmaɪkroʊˌkərn(ə)l| Computing a small modular part of an operating system kernel that implements its basic features [2].

The expression مَّا بَعُوضَةً فَمَا فَوْقَهَا can indicate all these complex systems in micro and smaller levels of small scales that humans have zeal to go further in research. Therefore, true engagement of science increases one's imān. A true scientist knows Allah ﷻ with true tawhid and true imān at the highest levels of certainty beyond the regular imān of ordinary people.

The Attitude: Imān or Kufr

It is interesting to analyze the sila word الَّذِينَ in the Qurān. This word denotes qualities, attributes and attitudes especially for humans. One of these attitudes denoted with الَّذِينَ is the attitude of imān and kufr. This is symmetrically mentioned with الَّذِينَ آمَنُواْ and الَّذِينَ كَفَرُواْ in the part of the ayah فَأَمَّا الَّذِينَ آمَنُواْ فَيَعْلَمُونَ أَنَّهُ الْحَقُّ مِن رَّبِّهِمْ وَأَمَّا الَّذِينَ كَفَرُواْ فَيَقُولُونَ مَاذَا أَرَادَ اللّهُ بِهَذَا مَثَلاً.

In other words, although here the example is a fly as mentioned with the word بَعُوضَةً, yet the underlying determining factor for imān or kufr is the attitude of the person.

When we analyze the gist of imān and kufr, one can realize both perspectives focusing on the attitude and perspective.

The attitude of humbleness and humility is prerequisite of imān. Humbleness and humility are the attitudes of acceptance after recognition and knowledge.

In other words, the attitude of humbleness and humility entail the following process:

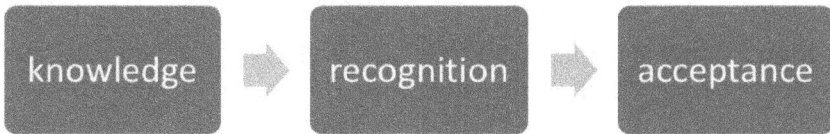

knowledge ➡ recognition ➡ acceptance

The opposite of this attitude is arrogance. The attitude of arrogance can entail

knowledge ➡ recognition ➡ rejection

When we compare above two diagrams in attitudes of imān and kufr or in the attitudes of humbleness/humility and arrogance, imān leads to acceptance, submission, peaceful states of taslim, Islām and being a Muslim.

The latter kufr leads to rejection, disobedience, chaotic states of darkness, and being a kafir.

Imān is structure, order, meaning and purpose. Kufr is chaos, purposelessness, doubts, and unending purposeless statistical arguments.

Imān relates everything with Allah ﷻ as mentioned as مِن رَّبِّهِمْ in this ayah as فَأَمَّا الَّذِينَ آمَنُواْ فَيَعْلَمُونَ أَنَّهُ الْحَقُّ مِن رَّبِّهِمْ. Kufr relates everything to all different possibilities of statistical arguments of unending, unfinished businesses, hanging as a disturbance of doubts, and skepticism as mentioned وَأَمَّا الَّذِينَ كَفَرُواْ فَيَقُولُونَ مَاذَا أَرَادَ اللّهُ بِهَذَا in the expression مَاذَا أَرَادَ اللّهُ بِهَذَا.

Reality of the Free Will, Divine Mercy and Divine Intervention

To support the approach of the above diagram, one can focus on the part of the ayah[38] {البقرة/26} وَمَا يُضِلُّ بِهِ إِلَّا الْفَاسِقِينَ. The people who are led to dalalah, misguidance, are the ones who have fisq referred as fāsiq. The source or reason of fisq is denial and rejection. Therefore, the blame is not on the Qurān but on themselves for their choice of rejection, and denial but not acceptance.

The presence and existence of misguidance as permitted and created by Allah ﷻ is part of the functional existence of free will. One cannot discuss the existence of free-will if a person wants to do something good or evil, but the causalities that are supposed to give the end result does not work or function. Then, the free-will notion becomes dysfunctional. The acquirement, kasb of free will in the realms of this world is real. Due to this functional reality of free-will as created by Allah ﷻ, there is the kasb, acquirement or existence of fasād as mentioned[39] ظَهَرَ الْفَسَادُ فِي الْبَرِّ {الروم/41} وَالْبَحْرِ بِمَا كَسَبَتْ أَيْدِي النَّاسِ لِيُذِيقَهُم بَعْضَ الَّذِي عَمِلُوا لَعَلَّهُمْ يَرْجِعُونَ. This ayah underlines the functional reality of the free will with the critical phrase of بِمَا كَسَبَتْ أَيْدِي النَّاسِ.

Yet, Allah ﷻ has always the Hikmah, Divine Wisdom and Mercy. One of the hikmahs of Divine Allowance of existence of fasad is that sometimes the apparent existence of fasad in personal and social lives can lead to people truly to Allah ﷻ as mentioned {الروم/41} لَعَلَّهُمْ يَرْجِعُونَ. Then, some people possibly may be guided with dalalah/misguidance looking incidents as mentioned مَثَلاً يُضِلُّ بِهِ كَثِيراً وَيَهْدِي بِهِ كَثِيراً.

Still, most of the time, due to the Divine Mercy and Fadl of Allah ﷻ, Allah ﷻ eliminates and minimizes the intended evil of the people with the mystery of Divine Intervention in order to maintain societies, systems and structures in order in the world and in the universe. This

---

38. Indeed, Allah is not timid to present an example—that of a mosquito or what is smaller than it. And those who have believed know that it is the truth from their Lord. But as for those who disbelieve, they say, "What did Allah intend by this as an example?" He misleads many thereby and guides many thereby. And He misleads not except the defiantly disobedient,
39. Corruption has appeared throughout the land and sea by [reason of] what the hands of people have earned so He may let them taste part of [the consequence of] what they have done that perhaps they will return [to righteousness].

is mentioned as[40] الَّذِينَ أُخْرِجُوا مِن دِيَارِهِم بِغَيْرِ حَقٍّ إِلَّا أَن يَقُولُوا رَبُّنَا اللَّهُ وَلَوْلَا دَفْعُ اللَّهِ النَّاسَ بَعْضَهُم بِبَعْضٍ لَّهُدِّمَتْ صَوَامِعُ وَبِيَعٌ وَصَلَوَاتٌ وَمَسَاجِدُ يُذْكَرُ فِيهَا اسْمُ اللَّهِ كَثِيرًا وَلَيَنصُرَنَّ اللَّهُ مَن يَنصُرُهُ إِنَّ اللَّهَ لَقَوِيٌّ عَزِيزٌ {الحج/40}. In this ayah, the statement وَلَوْلَا دَفْعُ اللَّهِ النَّاسَ بَعْضَهُم بِبَعْضٍ especially emphasizes this reality of Divine Merciful Intervention whether people realize it or not.

Yet, everyone will be judged truly with their intention by Allah ﷻ. Accordingly, for every choice rendered through one's free will, there is an accountability. May Allah ﷻ give us ikhlas, Amìn.

Investment: Imãn or Kufr

Businesses requires decision to move on in life. Businesses require clarity, explicitly and openness in contracts. The tricky perspectives finding holes in the contracts of legal perspectives are not the main purpose of policies, laws or principles of businesses, policies, systems or governments. The detailed legal wordings are due to peripheral issues of systems not being abused due to some minority of ill-intended people targeting not on the main purpose of these systems but focusing on the loopholes to abuse them.

In this sense, life is the biggest and the most important business of the person. The most valuable asset of the person is how one invests the perspective of life regardless of their length of life span.

If a person lives 20,30,40,50,60 or 70 years or more, how should he or she invest their perspectives in their assigned lifespan?

The occurrences in life engagements such as being successful, in failure, winning, losing, marriage, divorced, injured or health are all secondary compared to the first and primary initial establishment of the life perspective.

In this regard, there are two possibilities and not more than two in this life perspectives.

The first is being clear, simple, meaningful, straightforward, explicit and open. This implies order and structure.

---

40. [They are] those who have been evicted from their homes without right—only because they say, "Our Lord is Allah." And were it not that Allah checks the people, some by means of others, there would have been demolished monasteries, churches, synagogues, and mosques in which the name of Allah is much mentioned. And Allah will surely support those who support Him. Indeed, Allah is Powerful and Exalted in Might.

The second is being doubtful, complex, meaningless, chaotic, and endless implicit statistical arguments. This implies confusion and turmoil.

The first is called imān. Simple and straightforward and clear as "La ilaha illa Allah!".

The second is kufr. Endless darkness of zulumāt. Nothing is clear, explicit, and simple.

This absolute reality is mentioned as[41]

اللّهُ وَلِيُّ الَّذِينَ آمَنُواْ يُخْرِجُهُم مِّنَ الظُّلُمَاتِ إِلَى النُّورِ وَالَّذِينَ كَفَرُواْ أَوْلِيَآؤُهُمُ الطَّاغُوتُ يُخْرِجُونَهُم مِّنَ النُّورِ إِلَى الظُّلُمَاتِ أُوْلَئِكَ أَصْحَابُ النَّارِ هُمْ فِيهَا خَالِدُونَ {البقرة/257}

This simple and straightforward of absolute reality of La ilaha illa Allah is the relief, meaning, and light as mentioned اللّهُ وَلِيُّ الَّذِينَ آمَنُواْ يُخْرِجُهُم مِّنَ الظُّلُمَاتِ إِلَى النُّورِ.

The complex, so called "possible, illusion" or nowadays used in a wrong context of the word as "mystical" is very depressive, blur, stressful, and layers of darkness as mentioned وَالَّذِينَ كَفَرُواْ أَوْلِيَآؤُهُمُ الطَّاغُوتُ يُخْرِجُونَهُم مِّنَ النُّورِ إِلَى الظُّلُمَاتِ.

How can a person invest their most important asset of "the life perspective" on a non-understood, unpredicted, risky, doubtful, and no possible profit of a stock in a stock market called kufr?

This is called committing suicide of the business and it is not even called gambling. In gambling, there is a chance that the person can win. In this type of statistical arguments of doubts, skepticism and possibilities, the person is so much lost that they don't know really what they are doing and why they are adapting this life perspectives in terms of its gain and loss.

In a good business, the terms are clear, net, and the person minimizes all the risks as much as possible in the investment.

Then, one can really realize this notion repeatedly mentioned in the Qurān simply and clearly about this reality as[42]

أُوْلَئِكَ الَّذِينَ اشْتَرُوُاْ الضَّلاَلَةَ بِالْهُدَى فَمَا رَبِحَت تِّجَارَتُهُمْ وَمَا كَانُواْ مُهْتَدِينَ {البقرة/16}

---

41. Allah is the ally of those who believe. He brings them out from darknesses into the light. And those who disbelieve—their allies are Taghut. They take them out of the light
42. Those are the ones who have purchased error [in exchange] for guidance, so their transaction has brought no profit, nor were they guided.

إِنَّ اللَّهَ اشْتَرَى مِنَ الْمُؤْمِنِينَ أَنفُسَهُمْ وَأَمْوَالَهُم بِأَنَّ لَهُمُ الْجَنَّةَ يُقَاتِلُونَ فِي سَبِيلِ اللَّهِ فَيَقْتُلُونَ وَيُقْتَلُونَ وَعْدًا عَلَيْهِ حَقًّا فِي التَّوْرَاةِ وَالْإِنجِيلِ وَالْقُرْآنِ وَمَنْ أَوْفَى بِعَهْدِهِ مِنَ اللَّهِ فَاسْتَبْشِرُوا بِبَيْعِكُمُ الَّذِي بَايَعْتُم بِهِ وَذَلِكَ هُوَ الْفَوْزُ الْعَظِيمُ {التوبة/111} ⁴³

إِنَّ الَّذِينَ اشْتَرَوُا الْكُفْرَ بِالْإِيمَانِ لَن يَضُرُّوا اللَّهَ شَيْئًا وَلَهُمْ عَذَابٌ أَلِيمٌ {آل عمران/177} ⁴⁴

وَلَقَدْ أَخَذَ اللَّهُ مِيثَاقَ بَنِي إِسْرَائِيلَ وَبَعَثْنَا مِنهُمُ اثْنَيْ عَشَرَ نَقِيبًا وَقَالَ اللَّهُ إِنِّي مَعَكُمْ لَئِنْ أَقَمْتُمُ الصَّلَاةَ وَآتَيْتُمُ الزَّكَاةَ وَآمَنتُم بِرُسُلِي وَعَزَّرْتُمُوهُمْ وَأَقْرَضْتُمُ اللَّهَ قَرْضًا حَسَنًا لَّأُكَفِّرَنَّ عَنكُمْ سَيِّئَاتِكُمْ وَلَأُدْخِلَنَّكُمْ جَنَّاتٍ تَجْرِي مِن تَحْتِهَا الْأَنْهَارُ فَمَن كَفَرَ بَعْدَ ذَلِكَ مِنكُمْ فَقَدْ ضَلَّ سَوَاءَ السَّبِيلِ {المائدة/12} ⁴⁵

مَنْ ذَا الَّذِي يُقْرِضُ اللَّهَ قَرْضًا حَسَنًا فَيُضَاعِفَهُ لَهُ وَلَهُ أَجْرٌ كَرِيمٌ {الحديد/11} ⁴⁶

نَّ الْمُصَّدِّقِينَ وَالْمُصَّدِّقَاتِ وَأَقْرَضُوا اللَّهَ قَرْضًا حَسَنًا يُضَاعَفُ لَهُمْ وَلَهُمْ أَجْرٌ كَرِيمٌ {الحديد/18} ⁴⁷

May Allah ﷻ embody us with Imãn, Amìn

May Allah ﷻ protect us from any speck of the dust of the kufr, Amìn

Allahumma Salli Ala Sayyidina Wa Habibina Wa Mawlana Muhammad ﷺ al-Mustafa!

---

43. Indeed, Allah has purchased from the believers their lives and their properties [in exchange] for that they will have Paradise. They fight in the cause of Allah, so they kill and are killed. [It is] a true promise [binding] upon Him in the Torah and the Gospel and the Qur'an. And who is truer to his covenant than Allah? So rejoice in your transaction which you have contracted. And it is that which is the great attainment.

44. Indeed, those who purchase disbelief [in exchange] for faith—never will they harm Allah at all, and for them is a painful punishment.

45. And Allah had already taken a covenant from the Children of Israel, and We delegated from among them twelve leaders. And Allah said, "I am with you. If you establish prayer and give zakah and believe in My messengers and support them and loan Allah a goodly loan, I will surely remove from you your misdeeds and admit you to gardens beneath which rivers flow. But whoever of you disbelieves after that has certainly strayed from the soundness of the way."

46. Who is it that would loan Allah a goodly loan so He will multiply it for him and he will have a noble reward?

47. Indeed, the men who practice charity and the women who practice charity and [they who] have loaned Allah a goodly loan—it will be multiplied for them, and they will have a noble reward.

Types of Questions & Disagreement Statements

When we analyze the expression[48] وَأَمَّا الَّذِينَ كَفَرُواْ فَيَقُولُونَ مَاذَا أَرَادَ أُللَّه بِهَذَا مَثَلًا
يُضِلُّ بِهِ كَثِيراً وَيَهْدِي بِهِ كَثِيراً وَمَا يُضِلُّ بِهِ إلاَّ الْفَاسِقِينَ {البقرة/26}, there are some
critical points that reveal.

Our time of popular encouraged critical thinking methodology
by questioning and disagreement is implicitly mentioned in this ayah.
There are two perspectives or intentions in questions or statements
indicating disagreements.

One may have or may not have an idea about something. He or
she can ask a question to really clarify and to understand and learn
about it. The other is that one has already have an idea or thought about
something and may not have an idea about something. Yet, he or she
questions not to really learn, clarify or if his or her idea is right or wrong,
but they ask in order to confront, humiliate, challenge, force and impose
their thoughts on the other person.

The first case is the case of an open-minded person without any bias
and judgment seeking knowledge to learn. The second case is a narrow-
minded person with bias and judging others in order to brainwash
others.

The first case indicates empathy. The second case indicates
humiliating and mocking others.

Today's intolerances among different ethnic, religious, cultural or
gender groups are all related due to the attitude of the second group.

Disguise of Critical Thinking and Mass Misguidance

The approach of critical thinking and questioning is and has always been
a virtuous trait in the pursuit of true knowledge and the real absolute
needed knowledge on the journey of Allah ﷻ, referred as marifatullah.

The genuine question of angels to Allah ﷻ about the wisdom behind
the creation of humans with Adam as is one of the starting examples.
The genuine questions of Musa (عليه السلام) with Khidr are all some
examples of sincere efforts of learning.

---

48. Indeed, Allah is not timid to present an example—that of a mosquito or what is smaller
than it. And those who have believed know that it is the truth from their Lord. But as for those
who disbelieve, they say, "What did Allah intend by this as an example?" He misleads many
thereby and guides many thereby. And He misleads not except the defiantly disobedient,

In this sense, questioning with the intention of learning and increasing one's marifatullah is one of the, maybe, the highest traits as a tool on the path of Allah ﷻ.

Yet, munafiqs are defined as the kafir disguised in the form of a Muslim. Their level is worse than a kafir. Their harm to Muslims are worse than a kafir due to disguise of their internal with the good-looking external of being a Muslim.

Similarly, questions disguised with the virtuous traits of critical thinking is worse than the questions openly stating the rejection, confrontation or even humiliation. Therefore, the harms of logical-critical genuine looking questions are worse than open, and belligerent questions of shirk.

The first statement of this camouflaging is performed by Shaytān as "ana khayran minhu." Shaytān did not want to learn the wisdom of the creation of humans. He already had his judgment and bias with a camouflage in his reasoning of so called "virtuous critical thinking" as[49]

{ص/76} قَالَ أَنَا خَيْرٌ مِّنْهُ خَلَقْتَنِي مِن نَّارٍ وَخَلَقْتَهُ مِن طِينٍ

The latter case of approaches or questioning disguised under ingenuine perspectives can mislead the masses seeming to be logical but its inside is not genuine as mentioned in the Qurān in different places as mentioned in this ayah of Sûrah Baqarah as مَاذَا أَرَادَ اللَّهُ بِهَذَا مَثَلًا. Or in other ayahs in the Qurān as:[50]

وَقَالَ فِرْعَوْنُ يَا هَامَانُ ابْنِ لِي صَرْحًا لَّعَلِّي أَبْلُغُ الْأَسْبَابَ {غافر/36} أَسْبَابَ السَّمَاوَاتِ فَأَطَّلِعَ إِلَى إِلَهِ مُوسَى

وَقَالَ فِرْعَوْنُ يَا أَيُّهَا الْمَلَأُ مَا عَلِمْتُ لَكُم مِّنْ إِلَهٍ غَيْرِي فَأَوْقِدْ لِي يَا هَامَانُ عَلَى الطِّينِ فَاجْعَل لِّي صَرْحًا لَّعَلِّي أَطَّلِعُ إِلَى إِلَهِ مُوسَى وَإِنِّي لَأَظُنُّهُ مِنَ الْكَاذِبِينَ {القصص/38}[51]

When we review Firawn's statement, it initially gives the idea of genuine critical thinking as:

▶ يَا أَيُّهَا الْمَلَأُ مَا عَلِمْتُ لَكُم مِّنْ إِلَهٍ غَيْرِي: This is a strong statement of authority implying logic.

---

49. He said, "I am better than him. You created me from fire and created him from clay."
50. And Pharaoh said, "O Haman, construct for me a tower that I might reach the ways.
51. And Pharaoh said, "O eminent ones, I have not known you to have a god other than me. Then ignite for me, O Haman, [a fire] upon the clay and make for me a tower that I may look at the God of Moses. And indeed, I do think he is among the liars."

▶ فَأَوْقِدْ لِي يَا هَامَانُ عَلَى الطِّينِ فَاجْعَل لِّي صَرْحًا لَّعَلِّي أَطَّلِعُ إِلَى إِلَهِ مُوسَى : According to his logic, he wants to refute the claim of Musa (عليه السلام).

▶ لَأَظُنُّهُ مِنَ الْكَاذِبِينَ : Then, he uses an academic and logical reasoning of "I strongly think" with the word لَأَظُنُّهُ. This existence of takid in his statement actually implies that he already made his mind. Yet, he is still doing something that would not really change his mind.

If we analyze the flaw about his stance of not genuine learning but intending the approaches humiliation or judgment or bias, one can review other parts of the Qurān with the similar incident as below. This can also show their inconsistent, political or double-faced approaches:[52]

قَالَ فِرْعَوْنُ وَمَا رَبُّ الْعَالَمِينَ {الشعراء/23} قَالَ رَبُّ السَّمَاوَاتِ وَالْأَرْضِ وَمَا بَيْنَهُمَا إِن كُنتُم مُّوقِنِينَ {الشعراء/24} قَالَ لِمَنْ حَوْلَهُ أَلَا تَسْتَمِعُونَ {الشعراء/25} قَالَ رَبُّكُمْ وَرَبُّ آبَائِكُمُ الْأَوَّلِينَ {الشعراء/26} قَالَ إِنَّ رَسُولَكُمُ الَّذِي أُرْسِلَ إِلَيْكُمْ لَمَجْنُونٌ {الشعراء/27} قَالَ رَبُّ الْمَشْرِقِ وَالْمَغْرِبِ وَمَا بَيْنَهُمَا إِن كُنتُمْ تَعْقِلُونَ {الشعراء/28} قَالَ لَئِنِ اتَّخَذْتَ إِلَهًا غَيْرِي لَأَجْعَلَنَّكَ مِنَ الْمَسْجُونِينَ {الشعراء/29}

▶ قَالَ لِمَنْ حَوْلَهُ أَلَا تَسْتَمِعُونَ : Musa as presents a data. Then, Firawn does not engage with the content but he follows the attitude of humiliation.

▶ قَالَ إِنَّ رَسُولَكُمُ الَّذِي أُرْسِلَ إِلَيْكُمْ لَمَجْنُونٌ {الشعراء/27} : Then, Fira'wn increases his explicit humiliation due to possibly overwhelming increased logic of the content as present by Musa (عليه السلام).

▶ قَالَ لَئِنِ اتَّخَذْتَ إِلَهًا غَيْرِي لَأَجْعَلَنَّكَ مِنَ الْمَسْجُونِينَ {الشعراء/29} : As the Fir'awn does not really use logic and genuine method of questioning, learning and critical thinking, he threatens Musa (عليه السلام).

---

52. Said Pharaoh, "And what is the Lord of the worlds?" [Moses] said, "The Lord of the heavens and earth and that between them, if you should be convinced." [Pharaoh] said to those around him, "Do you not hear?" [Moses] said, "Your Lord and the Lord of your first forefathers." [Pharaoh] said, "Indeed, your 'messenger' who has been sent to you is mad." [Moses] said, "Lord of the east and the west and that between them, if you were to reason." [Pharaoh] said, "If you take a god other than me, I will surely place you among those imprisoned."

Yet, Musa (عليه السلام) in his approach still uses a very logical stance with composure after this threat and mentions:[53] قَالَ أَوَلَوْ جِئْتُكَ بِشَيْءٍ مُبِينٍ {الشعراء/30}. Since, Firawn seemed to be failed in the first part of the argument. He needs a logical seeming argument to disguise and make policies as mentioned[54] قَالَ لِلْمَلِإِ حَوْلَهُ إِنَّ هَذَا لَسَاحِرٌ عَلِيمٌ {الشعراء/34} يُرِيدُ أَن يُخْرِجَكُم مِّنْ أَرْضِكُم بِسِحْرِه فَمَاذَا تَأْمُرُونَ {الشعراء/35}

One can review today's six levels of policy making as that public should be convinced that this policy is needed either through cases studies, media coverage and expert opinion. Then, public reaction to new policies are constantly monitored if the policy will fail or pass [8]. I don't think there is much difference of public or mass related guidance or misguidance since the prior times such as Fir'awn until our times that there are different disciplines and fields that study policy making, governance, and political science.

When we today review the historical and today's mass evils such as the holocaust, mass-killings approved by policies of institutions or governments, there is so called a "virtuous seeming reason or critical thinking" justifying the evil. The effect and damage of this can be worse.

In this approach, one can make the masses to buy into the disguised form of evil behind the notions of reason and critical thinking. Then, they all can be this part of this mass-evil movement. The logical minority becomes suppressed, oppressed and terminated.

Unfortunately, when we look at the religious movements, political movements or other ones, this reality has been always there.

In the case of the legitimizing the creed of trinity in the counsel of Nicaea , the Unitarians were terminated and suppressed [9] under the so called critical thinking of "unification."

In the case of Rasulullah ﷺ, bringing a new teaching of tawhid, the early Meccans tried to legitimize their mass oppression by disguising behind the critical thinking of statements such as "we should be loyal to our forefathers religion, or this new teaching is separating the society and giving rights to the slaves, women and the poor. It is changing our norms" [10].

---

53. [Moses] said, "Even if I brought you proof manifest?"
54. [Pharaoh] said to the eminent ones around him, "Indeed, this is a learned magician. He wants to drive you out of your land by his magic, so what do you advise?"

Cycles of Mass Misguidance & Mass Guidance

After this mass misguidance through legitimized seeming policies or rules, Allah ﷻ gives hope to the believers that Allah ﷻ is always in control of people's guidance and misguidance according to their true stance regardless of their efforts temporary victories of mass misguidance of people.

This is notion is explicitly mentioned in many parts of the Qurān as:[55] وَكَانَ فِي الْمَدِينَةِ تِسْعَةُ رَهْطٍ يُفْسِدُونَ فِي الْأَرْضِ وَلَا يُصْلِحُونَ {النمل/48} قَالُوا تَقَاسَمُوا بِاللَّهِ لَنُبَيِّتَنَّهُ وَأَهْلَهُ ثُمَّ لَنَقُولَنَّ لِوَلِيِّهِ مَا شَهِدْنَا مَهْلِكَ أَهْلِهِ وَإِنَّا لَصَادِقُونَ {النمل/49} وَمَكَرُوا مَكْرًا وَمَكَرْنَا مَكْرًا وَهُمْ لَا يَشْعُرُونَ {النمل/50} فَانظُرْ كَيْفَ كَانَ عَاقِبَةُ مَكْرِهِمْ أَنَّا دَمَّرْنَاهُمْ وَقَوْمَهُمْ أَجْمَعِينَ {النمل/51} فَتِلْكَ بُيُوتُهُمْ خَاوِيَةً بِمَا ظَلَمُوا إِنَّ فِي ذَلِكَ لَآيَةً لِّقَوْمٍ يَعْلَمُونَ {النمل/52}

Especially, the sequence of the ayah as يُضِلُّ بِهِ كَثِيراً وَيَهْدِي بِهِ كَثِيراً in this Sûrah (26-Baqara) can indicate their initial seeming victory of mass-misguidance of people. Yet, the following part of وَيَهْدِي بِهِ كَثِيراً follows as the mass guidance of the people.

Today, in communication or media studies, there is the increased notion of "negative publicity" actually adds into publicity regardless of the types of publicity. In this sense, collective efforts of unification against Muslims globally can actually be the means for mass guidance of the people as part of the sunnatullah. This interpretation was mentioned repeatedly in different writings.

Sunnatullah

The cycles of mass misguidance and mass guidance can be also part of the sunnatullah. For example, the introduced creed of trinity with the counsel of Nicaea can be mass misguidance through policy making of forced unification, eliminating Unitarians. Yet, Isa alayhi salam coming before during the times of End of the Days and updating the creed of the Christianity to its original source can be the mass guidance of people in

---

55. And there were in the city nine family heads causing corruption in the land and not amending [its affairs]. They said, "Take a mutual oath by Allah that we will kill him by night, he and his family. Then we will say to his executor, 'We did not witness the destruction of his family, and indeed, we are truthful.'" And they planned a plan, and We planned a plan, while they perceived not. Then look how was the outcome of their plan—that We destroyed them and their people, all. So those are their houses, desolate because of the wrong they had done. Indeed in that is a sign for people who know.

the realms of sunnatullah as mentioned in the prophecy of Rasulullah ﷺ [3] (hadith #155).

Linguistically, the usage of the verb form of mudari (present/future) in the expression يُضِلُّ بِهِ كَثِيراً وَيَهْدِي for both يُضِلُّ and يَهْدِي can indicate this continuity (istimrār) indicating this notion as part of the sunnatullah.

Sunnatullah can indicate this cycling notions of causality encouraging people to work for the good, ethical, moral and justice related values in both personal and social lives. At the same time, sunnatullah can indicate this hope and full trust in Allah ﷻ when especially the reasons or cause-effects seem to be dysfunctional. This is by knowing and realizing that occurrences of everything is through sunnatullah with the Divine Will (Mashiyyah).

[27]

إِنَّ اللَّهَ لاَ يَسْتَحْيِي أَن يَضْرِبَ مَثَلاً مَّا بَعُوضَةً فَمَا فَوْقَهَا فَأَمَّا الَّذِينَ آمَنُواْ فَيَعْلَمُونَ أَنَّهُ الْحَقُّ مِن رَّبِّهِمْ وَأَمَّا الَّذِينَ كَفَرُواْ فَيَقُولُونَ مَاذَا أَرَادَ اللَّهُ بِهَذَا مَثَلاً يُضِلُّ بِهِ كَثِيراً وَيَهْدِي بِهِ كَثِيراً وَمَا يُضِلُّ بِهِ إِلاَّ الْفَاسِقِينَ {البقرة/26}[56]

الَّذِينَ يَنقُضُونَ عَهْدَ اللَّهِ مِن بَعْدِ مِيثَاقِهِ وَيَقْطَعُونَ مَا أَمَرَ اللَّهُ بِهِ أَن يُوصَلَ وَيُفْسِدُونَ فِي الأَرْضِ أُولَئِكَ هُمُ الْخَاسِرُونَ {البقرة/27}

One should remember that Allah ﷻ can give different examples in the Qurān. All the examples are real, exact, and have both very clear scientific, implicit and explicit and convoluted meanings. The people of imān approach to the Kalam of Allah ﷻ and Shi'ar of Allah ﷻ with adab.

The people of kufr or the people with attitudes of kufr approach to the shi'ar of Allah ﷻ without adab. Imān is adab. Fisq and kizb are kufr.

All the shi'ar of Allah ﷻ is expressed with الَّذِينَ يَنقُضُونَ عَهْدَ اللَّهِ مِن بَعْدِ مِيثَاقِهِ وَيَقْطَعُونَ. The expressions عَهْدَ اللَّهِ and مَا أَمَرَ اللَّهُ بِهِ can indicate all the shi'ar as outlined by Allah ﷻ and explained by Rasulullah ﷺ. Imān is the peak of this shi'ar that can be indicated in the expressions

---

56. Indeed, Allah is not timid to present an example—that of a mosquito or what is smaller than it. And those who have believed know that it is the truth from their Lord. But as for those who disbelieve, they say, "What did Allah intend by this as an example?" He misleads many thereby and guides many thereby. And He misleads not except the defiantly disobedient, Who break the covenant of Allah after contracting it and sever that which Allah has ordered to be joined and cause corruption on earth. It is those who are the losers.

عَهْدَ اللهِ and مَا أَمَرَ اللهُ بِهِ. All the haram and halāl are part of this shi'ar of Allah ﷻ.

In this regard, as the previous ayah ends with {الْفَاسِقِينَ 26/البقرة}, the following ayah details this fisq as[57] الَّذِينَ يَنْقُضُونَ عَهْدَ اللهِ مِن بَعْدِ مِيثَاقِهِ وَيَقْطَعُونَ. The result مَا أَمَرَ اللهُ بِهِ أَن يُوصَلَ وَيُفْسِدُونَ فِي الْأَرْضِ أُولَئِكَ هُمُ الْخَاسِرُونَ {البقرة/27} of all this fisq leads to a bad and sad ending as mentioned هُمُ الْخَاسِرُونَ {البقرة/27}.

At another perspective, the Qurān normalizes their fisq due to their perspectives of kufr and nifāq. In other words, when a person engages oneself with the engagements of kufr as mentioned الَّذِينَ يَنْقُضُونَ عَهْدَ اللهِ مِن بَعْدِ مِيثَاقِهِ, then chaos or fisq can be inevitable.

In this sense, عَهْدَ اللهِ can be anything related with true imān and tawhid of the person. Accordingly, عَهْدَ اللهِ can be also the sharia'h, rules and guidelines as presented through this imān and tawhid by the scriptures such as the Qurān, Tawrah or Injil and all the anbiya (عليهم السلام).

In this regard, Imān with its perspective of true tawhid and Islām with its rules and guidelines can indicate a totality of a perfect, harmonious, complete and complementary system as created, established, and maintained by Allah ﷻ. The problematic efforts of engagements either through belief and action can be considered as الَّذِينَ يَنْقُضُونَ عَهْدَ اللهِ مِن بَعْدِ مِيثَاقِهِ.

The word يَنْقُضُونَ can indicate a complex establish system. The negative efforts against this system can lead to chaos in both life perspectives of belief contrary to imān, and action contrary to amalu-salih as detailed by Islām. Allahu A'lam.

When we analyze the expression أُولَئِكَ هُمُ الْخَاسِرُونَ, the word أُولَئِكَ can indicate their farness from hidayah. This word أُولَئِكَ can also indicate the effort of distancing of Muslims from these qualities that lead to displeasure of Allah ﷻ. This word أُولَئِكَ can also indicate the difficulty of apparent and explicit feature of these qualities being not easily identifiable by others but the individual, him or herself knows it.

The pronoun هُمُ can indicate the specificity of these qualities to the people who embody these traits as mentioned الَّذِينَ يَنْقُضُونَ عَهْدَ اللهِ مِن بَعْدِ مِيثَاقِهِ وَيَقْطَعُونَ مَا أَمَرَ اللهُ بِهِ أَن يُوصَلَ وَيُفْسِدُونَ فِي الْأَرْضِ.

---

57. Who break the covenant of Allah after contracting it and sever that which Allah has ordered to be joined and cause corruption on earth. It is those who are the losers.

In other words, if a Muslim lose a business, trade or wealth, he or she is not considered as هُمُ الْخَاسِرُونَ in its literal understanding. The loss of Muslims in worldly engagements is not considered as a loss as the word الْخَاسِرُونَ generally is translated into English. The ones who are in real loss are the ones as mentioned الَّذِينَ يَنقُضُونَ عَهْدَ اللَّهِ مِن بَعْدِ مِيثَاقِهِ وَيَقْطَعُونَ مَا أَمَرَ اللَّهُ بِهِ أَن يُوصَلَ وَيُفْسِدُونَ فِي الْأَرْضِ. They are in loss in this world and in the afterlife.

[28]

كَيْفَ تَكْفُرُونَ بِاللَّهِ وَكُنتُمْ أَمْوَاتاً فَأَحْيَاكُمْ ثُمَّ يُمِيتُكُمْ ثُمَّ يُحْيِيكُمْ ثُمَّ إِلَيْهِ تُرْجَعُونَ {البقرة/28}[58]

[112]

بَلَى مَنْ أَسْلَمَ وَجْهَهُ لِلّهِ وَهُوَ مُحْسِنٌ فَلَهُ أَجْرُهُ عِندَ رَبِّهِ وَلاَ خَوْفٌ عَلَيْهِمْ وَلاَ هُمْ يَحْزَنُونَ {البقرة/112}[59]

Iman and Qadar: Taslìm & Inabah

One should remember that imãn in Allah ﷻ requires in imãn of Qadar of Allah ﷻ. Imãn to Qadar requires taslìm to Allah ﷻ in the verge of the events, incidents and happening.

This attitude of taslìm to Allah ﷻ leads to tawakkul. Tawawakkul leads to tawfiz. Both tawakkul and tawfiz take all the burden from the person's shoulder. There is no fear, worry, and anxiety. The person knows that Allah ﷻ is in charge of everything. He or she observes everything and tries to understand realities happening behind every incident with hikmah on the foundation of tawakkul to Allah ﷻ.

One should remember true inabah to Allah ﷻ comes after tawbah to Allah ﷻ. If turning to Allah ﷻ as tawbah is a state or hal, then the embodiment of tawbah as Inabah is a station or maqãm. Yet, true Taslim

---

58. How can you disbelieve in Allah when you were lifeless and He brought you to life; then He will cause you to die, then He will bring you [back] to life, and then to Him you will be returned.
59. Yes [on the contrary], whoever submits his face in Islam to Allah while being a doer of good will have his reward with his Lord. And no fear will there be concerning them, nor will they grieve.

comes after inabah as mentioned[60] وَأَنِيبُوا إِلَى رَبِّكُمْ وَأَسْلِمُوا لَهُ مِن قَبْلِ أَن يَأْتِيَكُمُ الْعَذَابُ ثُمَّ لَا تُنصَرُونَ {الزمر/54}. The true station of taslìm requires inabah.

Ibrahim (عليه السلام) and all the anbiya was constantly turning to Allah ﷻ as mentioned[61] وَقَالَ إِنِّي ذَاهِبٌ إِلَى رَبِّي سَيَهْدِينِ {الصافات/99}.

This constant inabah can make the person embody the station of taslìm.

Shirk and Taslim

إِذْ قَالَ لَهُ رَبُّهُ أَسْلِمْ قَالَ أَسْلَمْتُ لِرَبِّ الْعَالَمِينَ {البقرة/131}[62]

True imān requires true taslìm to Allah ﷻ in everything. The person giving a credit, share or any type of power on him or herself or anything else other than Allah ﷻ can engage in shirk.

Rabbul Alamìn is the One Who maintains, takes care of everything as long as the person understands and realizes this reality of taslìm.

All the types of absence of taslìm can lead to shirk. Each shirk can indicate darkness, pessimism, fear, anxiety.

Imān requires taslìm. Everything has imān and taslìm to Allah ﷻ except some unfortunate humans as mentioned[63]

أَفَغَيْرَ دِينِ اللَّهِ يَبْغُونَ وَلَهُ أَسْلَمَ مَن فِي السَّمَاوَاتِ وَالْأَرْضِ طَوْعًا وَكَرْهًا وَإِلَيْهِ يُرْجَعُونَ {آل عمران/83}

In this regard, in this ayah, وَلَهُ أَسْلَمَ مَن فِي السَّمَاوَاتِ وَالْأَرْضِ can indicate imān of all the beings in Allah ﷻ. Secondly, they also make full tawakkul and taslìm and tawfiz to Allah ﷻ.

In this regard, the skies, galaxies, planets, earth, moon, sun, and other entities fully understand, recognize and accept their fine and full dependency on Allah ﷻ. They fully make tawakkul to Allah ﷻ that they don't have fear of chaos, destruction and accidents.

---

60. And return [in repentance] to your Lord and submit to Him before the punishment comes upon you; then you will not be helped.
61. And [then] he said, "Indeed, I will go to [where I am ordered by] my Lord; He will guide me."
62. When his Lord said to him, "Submit", he said "I have submitted [in Islam] to the Lord of the worlds."
63. So is it other than the religion of Allah they desire, while to Him have submitted [all] those within the heavens and earth, willingly or by compulsion, and to Him they will be returned.

If sun, moon, earth, stars, planets, galaxies and all others have entities similar to most of the humans without taslìm, then they would be in constant fear of being destroyed, blasted and exploded.

Yet, these entities show their anger when some of these humans claim absence of taslìm, and claim shirk with Allah ﷻ as mentioned in the Qurān as[64] تَكَادُ السَّمَاوَاتُ يَتَفَطَّرْنَ مِنْهُ وَتَنشَقُّ الْأَرْضُ وَتَخِرُّ الْجِبَالُ هَدًّا {مريم/90}

أَن دَعَوْا لِلرَّحْمَنِ وَلَدًا {مريم/91}

Acceptance after Recognition and Taslim

فَإِنْ حَاجُّوكَ فَقُلْ أَسْلَمْتُ وَجْهِيَ لِلّهِ وَمَنِ اتَّبَعَنِ وَقُل لِّلَّذِينَ أُوتُواْ الْكِتَابَ وَالأُمِّيِّينَ أَأَسْلَمْتُمْ فَإِنْ أَسْلَمُواْ فَقَدِ اهْتَدَواْ وَّإِن تَوَلَّوْاْ فَإِنَّمَا عَلَيْكَ الْبَلاَغُ وَاللّهُ بَصِيرٌ بِالْعِبَادِ {آل عمران/20}[65]

One of the initial levels of taslìm is to accept what is reasonable and presented. When this acceptance is not present then, the next is arrogance. Arrogance leads rejection. Rejection leads to shirk.

This is also mentioned in other ayahs as[66] إِنَّا أَنزَلْنَا التَّوْرَاةَ فِيهَا هُدًى وَنُورٌ يَحْكُمُ بِهَا النَّبِيُّونَ الَّذِينَ أَسْلَمُواْ لِلَّذِينَ هَادُواْ وَالرَّبَّانِيُّونَ وَالأَحْبَارُ بِمَا اسْتُحْفِظُواْ مِن كِتَابِ اللّهِ وَكَانُواْ عَلَيْهِ شُهَدَاء فَلاَ تَخْشَوُاْ النَّاسَ وَاخْشَوْنِ وَلاَ تَشْتَرُواْ بِآيَاتِي ثَمَنًا قَلِيلاً وَمَن لَّمْ يَحْكُم بِمَا أَنزَلَ اللّهُ فَأُوْلَئِكَ هُمُ الْكَافِرُونَ {المائدة/44}

Muslim: The Real Embodiment of Taslim

In its true sense, the word Muslim is not a tag of a simple fan or club identity. It explains the quality of people with imān who have the quality of taslìm. Ibrahim(عليه السلام) was the example of Muslim. After all the external hardships such as being thrown in fire, Ibrahim as did not hesitate in his submission to Allah ﷻ. Both him and his son did not

---

64. The heavens almost rupture therefrom and the earth splits open and the mountains collapse in devastation That they attribute to the Most Merciful a son.

65. So if they argue with you, say, "I have submitted myself to Allah [in Islam], and [so have] those who follow me." And say to those who were given the Scripture and [to] the unlearned, "Have you submitted yourselves?" And if they submit [in Islam], they are rightly guided; but if they turn away—then upon you is only the [duty of] notification. And Allah is Seeing of [His] servants.

66. Indeed, We sent down the Torah, in which was guidance and light. The prophets who submitted [to Allah] judged by it for the Jews, as did the rabbis and scholars by that with which they were entrusted of the Scripture of Allah, and they were witnesses thereto. So do not fear the people but fear Me, and do not exchange My verses for a small price. And whoever does not judge by what Allah has revealed—then it is those who are the disbelievers.

hesitate in the attempted case of sacrifice for Allah ﷻ as mentioned[67] فَلَمَّا أَسْلَمَا وَتَلَّهُ لِلْجَبِينِ {الصافات/103}. Those are very difficult tests, trials and evil looking incidents as mentioned in the Qurān as[68] إِنَّ هَذَا لَهُوَ الْبَلَاءُ الْمُبِينُ {الصافات/106}. Yet, Ibrahim as established the institute of taslìm, tawakkul and tawfiz.

Yusuf as had a very difficult life. Everything was evil seeming. In the well, in the prison, and in different occasions, and in the incidents of modesty when he was blamed. Yet, he as asked Allah ﷻ to maintain this true state of imān as embodied with taslìm as a Muslim and die in this state. This is mentioned in the Qurān[69] رَبِّ قَدْ آتَيْتَنِي مِنَ الْمُلْكِ وَعَلَّمْتَنِي مِن تَأْوِيلِ الْأَحَادِيثِ فَاطِرَ السَّمَاوَاتِ وَالْأَرْضِ أَنتَ وَلِيِّي فِي الدُّنْيَا وَالْآخِرَةِ تَوَفَّنِي مُسْلِمًا وَأَلْحِقْنِي بِالصَّالِحِينَ {يوسف/101}.

Theodicy & Taslim

Then, the real point really boils down to the notions of today's discourses of theodicy, blaming God when a person faces an evil-looking incident.

This can show that the real test and trials hit the the person with attitude when and if examined with an evil-looking incident.

Then, there are two possible questions, perspectives or approaches:

▶ Does the person still maintain adab with Allah ﷻ and says "Let me see what the hikmah-wisdom behind this evil-looking incident is. Although I feel bitter about it, let me maintain my composure and attitude of acceptance for the Qadar of Allah ﷻ and ask ajir, reward for this indicent from Allah ﷻ with patience."

▶ Does the person lose adab with Allah ﷻ with the popularized ordinary problems of theodicy and say "how can this happen to me? I was trying to do everything right. What is the problem? Why me? I am so disturbed and angry."

May Allah ﷻ give us afiyah and easiness and attitude of Taslim to Allah ﷻ, Amin.

---

67. And when they had both submitted and he put him down upon his forehead,
68. Indeed, this was the clear trial.
69. My Lord, You have given me [something] of sovereignty and taught me of the interpretation of dreams. Creator of the heavens and earth, You are my protector in this world and in the Hereafter. Cause me to die a Muslim and join me with the righteous."

Our human realities are constantly mentioned in the Qurān about the absence of taslīm leading to shirk with the notions of theodicy, blame, and ingratitude with one's relations with Allah ﷻ. One of the examples is as[70] وَإِذَا مَسَّ الْإِنسَانَ ضُرٌّ دَعَا رَبَّهُ مُنِيبًا إِلَيْهِ ثُمَّ إِذَا خَوَّلَهُ نِعْمَةً مِّنْهُ نَسِيَ مَا كَانَ يَدْعُو إِلَيْهِ مِن قَبْلُ وَجَعَلَ لِلَّهِ أَندَادًا لِّيُضِلَّ عَن سَبِيلِهِ قُلْ تَمَتَّعْ بِكُفْرِكَ قَلِيلًا إِنَّكَ مِنْ أَصْحَابِ النَّارِ {الزمر/8}

Daily Events and Taslim

One should realize that our daily events constantly require the attitude of taslīm for a Muslim. Then, the person can handle the worries, stresses and challenges of each day, hour, and minute. The person can take the attitude of "oh Allah, I am weak. I submit myself to you with taslīm as a Muslim. Please make me embody true imān with taslīm. Make things easy for me. I am so weak. Don't put me in the pains and dark states of shirk. Keep in the light and sakina of imān with ihsan. Amīn"

Ihsan requires constant taslīm, tawakkul, and tawfiz. A few seconds of absence of ihsan and accordingly, absence of taslīm, tawakkul and tawfiz can place the person in the dark states of pessimism, hopelessness, anxiety and fear.

May Allah ﷻ never leave us with our own selves for even less than a blinking of an eye [11] (hadith 570#). Amīn.

Absence of Taslim and Self Oppression (Zulm) on the Nafs

قِيلَ لَهَا ادْخُلِي الصَّرْحَ فَلَمَّا رَأَتْهُ حَسِبَتْهُ لُجَّةً وَكَشَفَتْ عَن سَاقَيْهَا قَالَ إِنَّهُ صَرْحٌ مُّمَرَّدٌ مِّن قَوَارِيرَ قَالَتْ رَبِّ إِنِّي ظَلَمْتُ نَفْسِي وَأَسْلَمْتُ مَعَ سُلَيْمَانَ لِلَّهِ رَبِّ الْعَالَمِينَ {النمل/44}[71]

When a person does not embody true Islām as a Muslim that requires taslīm, then the person really oppresses their own selves.

---

70. And when adversity touches man, he calls upon his Lord, turning to Him [alone]; then when He bestows on him a favor from Himself, he forgets Him whom he called upon before, and he attributes to Allah equals to mislead [people] from His way. Say, "Enjoy your disbelief for a little; indeed, you are of the companions of the Fire."

71. She was told, "Enter the palace." But when she saw it, she thought it was a body of water and uncovered her shins [to wade through]. He said, "Indeed, it is a palace [whose floor is] made smooth with glass." She said, "My Lord, indeed I have wronged myself, and I submit with Solomon to Allah, Lord of the worlds."

The first oppression comes immediately in this world. He or she puts so much burden on their weak nafs that the nafs is placed in chaos, fear, pessimism, anger, anxiety and stress. The poor and weak nafs becomes dying and not spiritually breathing.

The whole field of psychology and psychiatry are founded on helping these unfortunate nafs or egos who have the absence of taslìm.

One should remember that absence of taslìm is all related with shirk, oppression to oneself. In this life perspective of shirk, kufr without taslìm to Allah ﷻ, the person really kills their own selves as if they shoot with a bullet to their own leg.

An outsider person of true imān and Islām with taslìm, when watching these sad situation of self-oppressors, he or she feels so much sad and bad for them and cries for them to help.

One should remember that the true engagements of spiritual help to others is not related with the cliché issues of missionary work. It is through helping people in order them not to oppress and hurt their own selves. Both spiritual and physical hurting are all related. A person, who is diagnosed with the cases of psychology and psychiatry, potentially can hurt their own selves spiritually and even sometimes, physically. Today's increasing addictions in drugs, and alcohol and trends of committing suicide can be some widespread examples of this problem.

[123]

وَاتَّقُواْ يَوْماً لاَّ تَجْزِي نَفْسٌ عَن نَّفْسٍ شَيْئاً وَلاَ يُقْبَلُ مِنْهَا عَدْلٌ وَلاَ تَنفَعُهَا شَفَاعَةٌ وَلاَ هُمْ يُنصَرُونَ {البقرة/123}[72]

Nafs in Between Qalb/Rûh and Shaytãn/Temptations

When we review the ayahs of the Qurãn the term nafs is repeated and emphasized in many places. In this regard, we have the soul-rûh or sometimes referred as (spiritual) heart-Qalb adhering to its fitrah, natural disposition of seeking for Allah ﷻ with La ilaha illa Allah. The only way of calmness, sakina, and itminãn, tranquility of the heart is

---

72. And fear a Day when no soul will suffice for another soul at all, and no compensation will be accepted from it, nor will any intercession benefit it, nor will they be aided.

with Allah ☀ and remembering Allah ☀ as mentioned[73] الَّذِينَ آمَنُواْ وَتَطْمَئِنُّ قُلُوبُهُم بِذِكْرِ اللّهِ أَلاَ بِذِكْرِ اللّهِ تَطْمَئِنُّ الْقُلُوبُ {الرعد/28}.

On the other hand, we have an entity called nafs, which is the means of application and reality encountering in this world.

In this sense, Qalb and Rûh are two entities engaging and interacting with beyond and high and Transcendent Reality of Allah ☀ with Dhikrullah.

Nafs is a reality engaging and interacting with the notions and realities of this world, an immediate accessible physical seen reality.

In this sense, one can think about Rûh and Qalb as the good and virtuous teachers. Shaytān and all attractions of the world can be the bad and evil teachers.

Nafs is the student under the influence of both of them. Nafs is the one that displays the execution under the command of Rûh/Qalb leading to Dhikrullah. Or, nafs can be under the command of shaytan and temptations leading to oppressing their own selves and others.

In the sense, nafs has a polar or linear position being pulled either on side or another as depicted below:

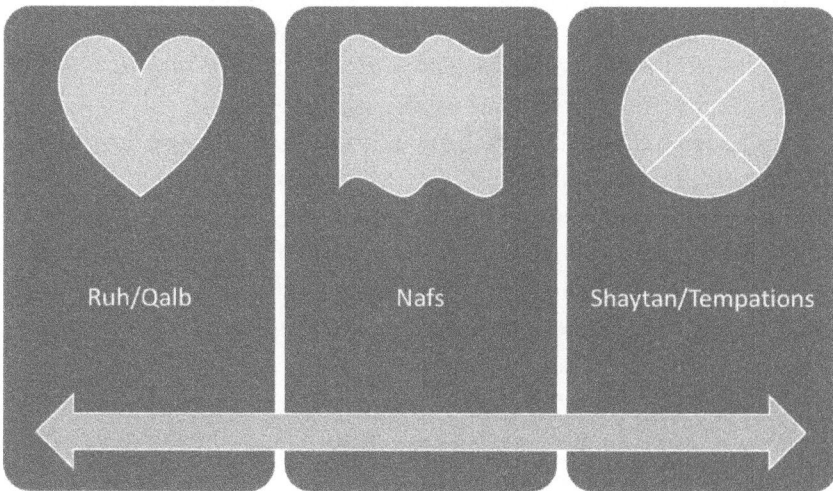

Ruh/Qalb   Nafs   Shaytan/Tempations

Nafs Being Pulled on the direction of Rûh/Qalb or Shaytān/ Temptations.

---

73. Those who have believed and whose hearts are assured by the remembrance of Allah. Unquestionably, by the remembrance of Allah hearts are assured."

Levels of Nafs

For some people, nafs can act like a wild animal that can destroy the things without guidance and with an impairment of the effects of the Rûh and Qalb. This wild nafs can be called nafs-ammarah.

For some people, through Dhikrullah, one can control the nafs through the teachings of the Rûh and Qalb as connected to the guidance of the Qurãn and Sunnah of Rasulullah ﷺ. This type of nafs can be called nafs lawwamah, nafs mutmainnah or nafs radiyah or mardiyyah depending on the level.

Nafs lawwamah can be initial stages of the control. Nafs still makes a lot of mistakes under the influence of Shaytãn and worldly temptations. Yet, the nafs in this person recognizes their mistake and constantly goes back to Allah ﷻ for forgiveness. This cycle continues may be until one dies. Then, the person may end their journey still in a positive state with the forgiveness of Allah ﷻ, Insha Allah. In this type of nafs, Rûh and Qalb constantly warns the person and the person still knows the true teachings of them. Yet, he or she still follows on and off these teachings, regrets and goes back to Allah ﷻ.

Nafs Mutmainnah has a better control of the nafs that he or she does not complain any of the evil-seeming incidents and he does not become arrogant with good-seeming incidents. He tries to keep the same level of zuhd, detachment but connects to La ilaha illa Allah. In this case, Qalb and Rûh has a higher effect on the nafs. Nafs strictly follows the teachers of Qalb and Rûh with dhikrullah without much paying attention to the renderings of Shaytãn and tempetations.

Nafs Radiyah is a state of the nafs that Qalb and nafs seeks the rida of Allah ﷻ. In this regards, the insructions that come to the nafs is all along the rida of Allah ﷻ with full ikhlas. In this regard, rather than the quantity, quality can matter more.

Nafs Mardiyyah is the state of the nafs that Allah ﷻ approves with the Divine Rida. In this regard, even the shaytan/jinn or tempatiton of the person become Muslim. This can be the nafs of the elects such as Rasulullah ﷺ. This is the type of a nafs that if Shaytãn still tries to challenge this nafs, Shaytãn can endanger his life as Shaytãn tried to disturb Rasulullah ﷺ during the tahajjud, he was caught by Rasulullah ﷺ. Rasulullah ﷺ did not execute the punishment on him due his mercy and respect for another elect of this nafs, Sulayman as for his sole request

قَالَ رَبِّ اغْفِرْ لِي وَهَبْ لِي مُلْكًا لَّا يَنبَغِي لِأَحَدٍ مِّنْ بَعْدِي إِنَّكَ أَنتَ 74:as ۞ from Allah
الْوَهَّابُ {ص/35}

This is a level of nafs as nafs mardiyyah, the shayatin becomes under control, nullified and becomes the servants as mentioned[75] فَسَخَّرْنَا لَهُ الرِّيحَ تَجْرِي بِأَمْرِهِ رُخَاء حَيْثُ أَصَابَ {ص/36} وَالشَّيَاطِينَ كُلَّ بَنَّاء وَغَوَّاصٍ {ص/37}

The Qalb of these elect inviduals of nafs-mardiyyah, especially the prophets, have the state of salìm as mentioned[76] إِلَّا مَنْ أَتَى اللَّه بِقَلْبٍ سَلِيمٍ {الشعراء/89}.

As one grows, in controlling one's nafs through the teachings of the Qalb and rûh, the Divine Openings with Grace and Fadl inreases as mentioned by Imam Ghazali [12]. In this sense, control of the Shayatin is the example of the Divine Openings with Grace and Fadl for the people of nafs mardiyyah from Allah ۞. For each level of nafs, there can be different openings from Allah ۞ with Grace and Fadl.

Nafs and Mind

If we focus on the nafs with its interaction with mind, one can say that the brain of the nafs is mind. In other words, mind is the essence of the nafs. Nafs executes decisions with mind, decision making under the conditions of free-will and free-choice.

A person who is not under the control of rûh and Qalb with the guidance of the Qurān and Sunnah of Rasulullah ۞ but under some control of the mind can still have some type of control of the nafs.

The effects of this control of the nafs only through mind without the imān, Qurān and sunnah of Rasulullah ۞ can have some effects in this world as the part of the following the sunnatullah, disciplines of science or psychology or cognitive sciences others.

The effects of yogis on the body through the trainings of the nafs with mind, popularized mindful studies in today's secular socieities, and others are some examples of the nafs under the training of the mind.

In these trainings or teachings, the most critical difference between Dhikrullah, a guidance from the Qurān and Sunnah (or Abrahamic religions in its general form including other traditions as sent by

---

74. He said, "My Lord, forgive me and grant me a kingdom such as will not belong to anyone after me. Indeed, You are the Bestower."
75. So We subjected to him the wind blowing by his command, gently, wherever he directed, And [also] the devils [of jinn]—every builder and diver
76. But only one who comes to Allah with a sound heart."

Allah ﷻ), and mindful or yogi related (stemming from present eastern religious traditions) the intention, explicitness and afterlife.

In the first case of imān and Islām, the intention is that one can bear the difficulties as prayers, rituals, fasting or sacrifice to please Allah ﷻ. In the other case, one can do all these as a training of pain of the self or body for the present time or life.

In the first case, Allah ﷻ as La ilaha illa Allah is explicit, simple and clear. In the latter case, a very blur language is used with science, scientific laws, or nature to implicitly deify or idolize something.

In the first case, accountability, afterlife and expectations are clear and structured. In the later case, the afterlife and accountability concepts are not clear but based on ideas assumptions or opinions.

In the first case, the source of the knowledge is from Allah ﷻ, the Transedent reality with the authentic scriptures. In the second case, it is the human's idea, comments and interpretations.

Some of today's Abrahamic religions having not a clear idea of afterlife or accountability such as Judaism is due to the effect of these philosophies on the traditional and authentic teachings of Judaism.

[130]

وَمَن يَرْغَبُ عَن مِّلَّةِ إِبْرَاهِيمَ إِلاَّ مَن سَفِهَ نَفْسَهُ وَلَقَدِ اصْطَفَيْنَاهُ فِي الدُّنْيَا وَإِنَّهُ فِي الآخِرَةِ لَمِنَ الصَّالِحِينَ {البقرة/130} [77]

Abrahamic Religions

Today, we use the term of Abrahamic religions to indicate Judaism, Christianity, and Islām. The Qurān mentions the collective body of scriptural based religions with the expression مِّلَّةِ إِبْرَاهِيمَ. In this sense, the term millata Ibrahim can indicate or allude or be replaced with Abrahamic religions in different contexts.

One of the indication of collective body of today's terminology of Abrahamic religions is that there is a scripture as Bible, Gospel, Torah, or the Qurān that explicitly mentions the communication between God, the One, Adonai, or as we refer as Allah ﷻ and humans. In this

---

77. And who would be averse to the religion of Abraham except one who makes a fool of himself. And We had chosen him in this world, and indeed he, in the Hereafter, will be among the righteous.

communication of scriptures, the purpose of life is explicitly explained with the teachings of some unseen realities after death and in our present life.

The Qurān mentions and can indicate that the right methodology is to follow an authentic scriptural guidance as outlined and transferred one generation or millennium to another with the guidance of prophets and scriptures sent by Allah ﷻ.

This collective tradition and methodology of approach to the religion is called Abrahamic religions or مَّلِةِ إِبْرَاهِيمَ.

The Qurān explicitly mentions that this is the correct methodology for identifying religion, or spiritulity to follow as mentioned وَمَن يَرْغَبُ عَن مَّلِةِ إِبْرَاهِيمَ إِلاَّ مَن سَفِهَ.

Mindful Studies, Buddhism & Abrahamic Religions

When we today consider and review classification of religions as Abrahamic versus non-Abrahamic ones, there is an interesting phenomenon that emerges. This phenomenon is historical, but its representations are becoming more dominant and explicit with today's mass communication means and liberalism notions of freedom.

There are people especially in the West isolating themselves from their parental exposed religions of Christianity and Judaism.

These isolated people in masses at different levels of intellectuality try to fulfil the need of religion in different ways.

The first is idolizing science by giving implicit divine or deistic meanings and expectations from nature, universe and anything around the words of science.

The emerging notions of philosophers as the founders of these ideas have formed different disciplines especially in social sciences.

In these efforts, the words secular become highly popular to alienate religion from daily and public life.

In all these alinations, the need for religion and Allah ﷻ is and has been always there for all humans from the creation of Adam (عليه السلام). These efforts of alienation people from Abrahamic religions especially Christinaity and Judaism generated new implicit deisitic terms such as science, nature, and others.

These alienations generated and popularized people with the tags as atheist, agnostic and none.

In one perspective, the people still carried the feelings and emotions of the need for Allah ﷻ.

Due to this run-away from Abrahamic religions, a new terminology "spiritual" or "spirituality" has become more popular.

With the same push and trends of this run away from Abrahamic religions, people are still hungry to fulfill their need for Allah ﷻ, there has been a focus on what is so called referred as non-Abrahamic or non-Deistic religions of native religions or Eastern such as Buddhisms, Hinduism (partially), Confucianism, Taoism and others.

Out of all the choices of these Western run-aways, Buddhism has become an alternative due to its established structure.

It is funny that the people who were running away from structure, order, and so-called institutionalized religions, they find refuge in another structured religion referred as "Buddhism". Since the term "religion" was a bad term for them, the term religion was replaced as phiolosophy for Buddhism.

In this regard, our run-aways were not really following a religion but it was a philosophy. They were happy because they are following a religion but they didn't call it as religion but philosophy.

Yet, in its essence, Buddhism has one of the detailed structured levels of respect among teacher and student relationships, parent children relationships and spousal relationships and others. I believe this is very important. Therefore, buddhism has survived. Yet, this was really dismissed by the ones who run away from the Western religions.

Then, these run-aways in the West started practicing Buddhism in their personal lifes as a need. Then, they tried to help people by emphasizing the secular and philophy perspective of Buddhism. The emerging fields of mindful studies in psychology, and yoga centers in churches and public spaces become so popular.

There is nothing wrong about helping people with different mindful practices and spiritual practices if is going to help people.

Yet, every tradition can offer these relevant and useful practices for all humans.

Yet, demonizing Abrahamic religions in intellectual renderings of college teachings and other avenues of intellectual circles leading the masses with media is not a fair approach of justice and non-discriminatory practices of our society.

It is also funny that Budha was believed to be one of the prophets of Allah ﷻ according to some scholars [13]. In this sense, one can really explain the notions of tazkiya, or tasawwuf have some relevance with current Buddhist teachings of eightfold path and other parts of its structured teachings. In this regard, Buddha or Siddartha Gautama (c.563– c.460 bc) can be part of the Abrahamic traditions as Ibrahim as lived much before than time of Siddartha Gautama.

The Explicit Need for Allah ﷻ and the Guidance of Scriptures and Prophets

The term Abrahamic religions indicate the explicit, clear and direct guidance of Allah ﷻ for all humans through the vehicle of scriptures and the prophets. In this sense, Abrahamic religions indicate this clear sunnatullah that has been present from the first creation of humans. The term Abrahamic religions or مِلَّةِ إِبْرَاهِيمَ can indicate this correct methodology of a person choosing, following and adapting a religion.

In this regard, a person adapts and follows a clear religion that is authenticated by Allah ﷻ. It is not an issue of personal feelings of choice only but if we are trying to engage ourselves to connect our emotions, soul, and spiritual heart to the One Who is Transcendent, then this connection should be a connection that is also approved, pleased and authenticated by Allah ﷻ.

Especially, this authentication and acceptance by Allah ﷻ becomes more critical when a person takes religion, spirituality, or mindfulness as a way of life but not as a one-time event.

Religion fulfilling our emotions, soul and spirituality is a need. It is not an optional engagement. Therefore, its authentication who gave us this need to connect to the One is very critical.

If we really analyze the expression[78] وَمَن يَرْغَبُ عَن مِّلَّةِ إِبْرَاهِيمَ إِلَّا مَن سَفِهَ نَفْسَهُ, then this expression can explicitly indicate the methodology of following a scripture, and a prophet with the expression مِلَّةِ إِبْرَاهِيمَ. This is today can be called Abrahamic religions.

Yet, this explicit structure is the key in scriptures and in Abrahamic religions. The explicitness of the teachings sent by Allah ﷻ, or referred as God or Adonai. The explicity of expectations, the explicitness of afterlife

---

78. And who would be averse to the religion of Abraham except one who makes a fool of himself.

and other parts are mentioned explicitly in the Qurān and sunnah of Rasulullah ﷺ.

One of the hikmah or wisdom of risalah, and presence of Rasulullah ﷺ and the Qurān is due to the blurriness in the teachings of Christianity and Judaism. This blurriness has been induced overtime and the issues of authenticity become questionable. In this regard, the Qurān does not tell people to live prior identities as Christians or Jews but tells them to update what they already have and remove the blurriness as mentioned

[286]

لاَ يُكَلِّفُ اللّهُ نَفْسًا إِلاَّ وُسْعَهَا لَهَا مَا كَسَبَتْ وَعَلَيْهَا مَا اكْتَسَبَتْ رَبَّنَا لاَ تُؤَاخِذْنَا إِن نَّسِينَا أَوْ أَخْطَأْنَا رَبَّنَا وَلاَ تَحْمِلْ عَلَيْنَا إِصْرًا كَمَا حَمَلْتَهُ عَلَى الَّذِينَ مِن قَبْلِنَا رَبَّنَا وَلاَ تُحَمِّلْنَا مَا لاَ طَاقَةَ لَنَا بِهِ وَاعْفُ عَنَّا وَاغْفِرْ لَنَا وَارْحَمْنَآ أَنتَ مَوْلاَنَا فَانصُرْنَا عَلَى الْقَوْمِ الْكَافِرِينَ {البقرة/286}[79]

Endurance Capacity-Taklīf

When we analyze the above ayah, Allah ﷻ mentions that in the mystery of human creation there can be two dominant Names and Attributes of Allah ﷻ.

One is al-Adl. Allah ﷻ is all Just and Fair. The statement in this as لاَ يُكَلِّفُ اللّهُ نَفْسًا إِلاَّ وُسْعَهَا لَهَا مَا كَسَبَتْ وَعَلَيْهَا مَا اكْتَسَبَتْ.

The other dominant Name and Attribute of Allah ﷻ besides al-Adl, the All Just is al-Rahman and al-Rahìm, the Most Merciful, the Most Graceful. Al-Rahman and al-Rahìm are constantly repeated in the beginning of each Sûrah and twice in the opening Sûrah, al-Fatiha. In this ayah, the parts رَبَّنَا لاَ تُؤَاخِذْنَا إِن نَّسِينَا أَوْ أَخْطَأْنَا رَبَّنَا وَلاَ تَحْمِلْ عَلَيْنَا إِصْرًا كَمَا حَمَلْتَهُ عَلَى الَّذِينَ مِن قَبْلِنَا رَبَّنَا وَلاَ تُحَمِّلْنَا مَا لاَ طَاقَةَ لَنَا بِهِ can indicate these two Names and Attributes of Allah ﷻ as al-Rahman and al-Rahìm, the Most Merciful, the Most Graceful.

One can deduce even from the analysis of this ayah that these two Names and Attributes of Allah ﷻ al-Rahman and al-Rahìm, the Most

---

79. Allah does not charge a soul except [with that within] its capacity. It will have [the consequence of] what [good] it has gained, and it will bear [the consequence of] what [evil] it has earned. "Our Lord, do not impose blame upon us if we have forgotten or erred. Our Lord, and lay not upon us a burden like that which You laid upon those before us. Our Lord, and burden us not with that which we have no ability to bear. And pardon us; and forgive us; and have mercy upon us. You are our protector, so give us victory over the disbelieving people."

Merciful, the Most Graceful are more dominant than the Name and Attribute of Allah ﷻ as al- Adl, the All Just.

Justice and fairness require لَهَا مَا كَسَبَتْ وَعَلَيْهَا مَا اكْتَسَبَتْ.

Yet, the overriding Name and Attribute of Allah ﷻ as Ar-Rahman and Ar-Rahìm, the Most Merciful, the Most Graceful and the Most Forgiving shows رَبَّنَا لاَ تُؤَاخِذْنَا إِن نَّسِينَا أَوْ أَخْطَأْنَا.

Therefore, the attitude of وَاعْفُ عَنَّا وَاغْفِرْ لَنَا وَارْحَمْنَآ أَنتَ مَوْلاَنَا can really indicate the expected position of a person that whatever he or she does regardless of their amount of sin, mistakes and oppression, when they go turn to Allah ﷻ with humbleness, humility, regret and ikhlas, sincerity, Allah ﷻ forgives and does not make the person accountable similar to human rational based accounting systems. Moreover so, Allah ﷻ can erase all the mistakes and errors of the person and turn into reward if the person makes a tawbah nasuhah.

Another perspective of these two Names and Attributes of Allah ﷻ as al-Adl and Ar-Rahmān and Ar-Rahìm present in our reality of being in tests and trials. These tests and trials can be called also as taklìf as mentioned لاَ يُكَلِّفُ اللّهُ نَفْسًا.

Taklìf can be the tests and trials of a person in the world or their real expected responsibility as a human in the earth.

Yet, even in these tests and trials, Allah ﷻ mentions that the Name and Attribute of Allah ﷻ can display as لاَ يُكَلِّفُ اللّهُ نَفْسًا إِلاَّ وُسْعَهَا. Every individual, self and human can have a different capacity of taking the responsibility and bearing tests, trials and tribulations in life. Allah ﷻ does not allow these trials, tests, tribulations or taklif to go over the limit of each person's capacity of endurance. This is the manifestation of the Name and Attribute of Allah ﷻ as al-Adl.

On the other hand, Allah ﷻ is ar-Rahmān and ar-Rahìm. Even though the person can try to handle tests and trials according to his or her capacity, one can try to appeal to an easy life with less or minimal tests and trials through the Name and Attribute of Allah ﷻ as ar-Rahmān and ar-Rahìm as mentioned رَبَّنَا وَلاَ تَحْمِلْ عَلَيْنَا إِصْرًا كَمَا حَمَلْتَهُ عَلَى الَّذِينَ مِن قَبْلِنَا رَبَّنَا وَلاَ تُحَمِّلْنَا مَا لاَ طَاقَةَ لَنَا بِهِ.

Sometimes, due to person's weakness or approaching to the limits of their capacity, one can really be affected with the trials and tests. He or she may lose their sleep. One can see nightmares at night. One can carry constant anxiety, worry, uneasiness and sadness due to the problems in his or her life or due to the problems happening around this person.

In this case, and all the time, taking refuge and running back to Allah ﷻ and in Allah ﷻ is extremely critical, essential and paramount. At these times, if we try to calm ourselves with other means, then our problems can increase and multiply further. If we try to discharge ourselves in Dhikrullah with crying, dua, salāh, istigfār, tasbīh, hamd, and the Qurān, then one can positively enlarge one's capacity of endurance or can realize or enjoy their real endurance capacity as given by Allah ﷻ in the realms of taklīf as the Name and Attribute of Allah ﷻ al-Adl can indicate.

Especially, if the person endures these problems with the intention of pleasing Allah ﷻ or if these problems are related about the concerns of other Muslims, and about concerns of the imān of all humanity, then the person can be a candidate for a noble zeal and desire similar to the prophets as mentioned[80] فَلَعَلَّكَ بَاخِعٌ نَّفْسَكَ عَلَى آثَارِهِمْ إِن لَّمْ يُؤْمِنُوا بِهَٰذَا الْحَدِيثِ أَسَفًا .لَعَلَّكَ بَاخِعٌ نَّفْسَكَ أَلَّا يَكُونُوا مُؤْمِنِينَ {الشعراء/3}[81] and {الكهف/6}

In the case of Rasulullah ﷺ as our model, he ﷺ was also in the endless limits of his capacity of endurance as he was carrying this worry and concern as mentioned above.

Yet, these worries and concerns can be appreciated by Rabbul Alamīn ﷻ.

Yet, one should remember that as Rasulullah ﷺ was in the state of being in constant and endless worry of others imān, he ﷺ was still maintaining a livable and social life with others. He did not reveal his real self of worry, and concern for others in its real and full capacity in order not to overwhelm people due to their lesser endurance capacity, taklīf.

In this regard, he ﷺ mentioned "if you knew what I knew, you would run away from your homes and families to the mountains," [14] (hadith 6485#).

This is again another reality of his endurance capacity and how to maintain and balance and contextualize within the notions of being in balance.

There are even a lot of ahlullah, the people of Allah ﷻ, when they have these overwhelming times of reaching to their endurance capacity

---

80. Then perhaps you would kill yourself through grief over them, [O Muhammad], if they do not believe in this message, [and] out of sorrow.
81. Perhaps, [O Muhammad], you would kill yourself with grief that they will not be believers.

of taklîf, they may run to the mountains or seclusion states of isolation. They may lose sometimes controlling these overwhelming internal struggles when encountering and facing with lower or lesser level human realities.

Yet, in these regards, and at all times for all level people on the path of Allah ﷻ, this reality is critical as[82] رَبَّنَا لَا تُؤَاخِذْنَا إِن نَّسِينَا أَوْ أَخْطَأْنَا رَبَّنَا وَلَا تَحْمِلْ عَلَيْنَا إِصْرًا كَمَا حَمَلْتَهُ عَلَى الَّذِينَ مِن قَبْلِنَا رَبَّنَا وَلاَ تُحَمِّلْنَا مَا لاَ طَاقَةَ لَنَا بِهِ وَاعْفُ عَنَّا وَاغْفِرْ لَنَا وَارْحَمْنَآ أَنتَ مَوْلاَنَا فَانصُرْنَا عَلَى الْقَوْمِ الْكَافِرِينَ {البقرة/286}.

Knowing One's Own Capacity and Working around it

As we always try to aim high in our relation with Allah ﷻ, knowing oneself and one's own capacity can be critical not to lose on the path of gain. In other words, as one can ask and beg for the highest level from Allah ﷻ on taqwa, our human realities can dictate to know our limits at a specific time, place and context. Rasulullah ﷺ is our practical example and model to embody in implementing these high aimed goals with practical means. Rasulullah ﷺ maintained a social and livable and smiling, gentle, caring and welcoming embodiment while he ﷺ was at another level of endurance of his capacity of worry and concern for the imãn of all.

For example, knowing one's own capacity requires that if he or she would be affected negatively due to some overwhelming problems. Possibly, in this case, the person should not volunteer to engage him or herself and listen. In this topic, we are not mentioning the issues of a person trying to learn that is not concern for them. No, here the discussion is the person can help others possibly but yet, he may lose himself during or at the end of this process spiritually in his or her endurance capacity. The signs of a person losing him or herself can be becoming pessimistic due to overwhelming problems, losing hope, and engaging oneself with theodicy leading to not to have a proper adab and good zann with Allah ﷻ. In these cases, purposeful avoidance for the sake of a higher good can be a solution.

---

82. Allah does not charge a soul except [with that within] its capacity. It will have [the consequence of] what [good] it has gained, and it will bear [the consequence of] what [evil] it has earned. "Our Lord, do not impose blame upon us if we have forgotten or erred. Our Lord, and lay not upon us a burden like that which You laid upon those before us. Our Lord, and burden us not with that which we have no ability to bear. And pardon us; and forgive us; and have mercy upon us. You are our protector, so give us victory over the disbelieving people."

If a person finds himself in a situation like this, first the person should ask constant help of Allah ﷻ for himself or herself for others as well, then try to minimize the effects of this problem by purposeful distancing and isolating themselves from the core narratives of the problem. Yet, making dua for the people who are in affliction, and helping them financial or physically to these persons of in need without going into psychological counseling part of the problem are still necessary. This approach can be essential, goal-oriented, fruitful both for the helper and the helped one. The helper can continue to help. The helped one can continue to receive the help. If the helper gets depressed and become pessimistic, he or she cannot help the ones in need if proper endurance capacity related monitoring is not performed.

Today, in modern counseling of academic perspectives, counseling is equal to listening [15].

Here, the key is that one should not volunteer to listen the narratives of a problem as a part of the psychological counseling if his or her endurance capacity is already shaky in the limits of spiritual shattering states. Yet, he or she can still direct these effected/traumatic individuals to a higher level of spiritual rank, professional counselors to help for counseling. At the same time, he or she can help these effected person or people with all means without going into the details of counseling.

Protecting the Valuables: Endurance Capacities of Taklīf and Imān

One should understand both taklīf and imān are directly related. In other words, the endurance capacities of a person against the tests and trials referred as taklīf and the level or endurance capacity of one's imān are directly related.

One cannot risk their own imān by indulging oneself by challenging their capacities of imān.

In this sense, one cannot say or do "let me review the Western discourses of philosophy, religion, deity how to they oppose the pillars of imān," if they don't have a purpose do this and their imān endurance capacity is not suitable to this, then this is a very nonsense engagement.

Actually, this approach can be similar to a child having a million dollar but does not care about protecting it. Similarly, true imān with tawhid is the most valuable asset of the person. Depending on the level of the person, this imān can be transferred from parents as the taqlidi, inherited valuable. Or, it can be gained and built with reason and logic. Both are with the Fadl and Grace of Allah ﷻ. Both are valuables depending on the level of the person.

A person of taqlidi imān or a person of not fully tahkiki imān should not dive into the fine details of evolution theory, or other skeptical approaches of philosophy. They can just waste their valuable of imān regardless of its quantity and quality.

Today, alienation from religion and increasing notions of theodicy without having proper adab and good-zann with Allah ﷻ is due to the approach of not valuing imān, the most valuable asset of the person.

Similarly, one should not engage himself in the responsibilities of taklif, if there are possible problems that can affect the imān of the person.

An improper assessment of one's own capacity of taklif can affect negatively one's imān. Therefore, things leading to pessimism, losing hope, worldviews of chaos, destruction and darkness are all implicit or covered layers of kufr, disbelief and unappreciation to Allah ﷻ.

Pessimism, hopelessness, and chaos are all in claim that everything is random but not in the Full Control of the Most Merciful, All-Living, All-Alive, the Sustainer and Order Establisher of the Universes, Allah ﷻ.

Hope, optimism, positive thinking, order and structure are all part of the imān to Allah ﷻ Who Creates, and Maintains everything.

Therefore, any engagement that would lead the person to these dark avenues of kufr through pessimism, hopelessness, and theodicy can work oppositely to one's imān.

One should give hope to others in the limits of capacity of one's imān. Yet, it should not at the expense of sacrificing it but still protecting the most valuable asset of imān and trying to help within these limits.

A good business will go bankruptcy if they give their asset as donation. They can donate their profits as much as they want as long as the main assets for the pillars are there. Even, because of donations they can make more money with a good intention. Similarly, one can help others within the allowance of their extras or profit in the treasures of their capacity as long as the pillars of imān, the main assets are there.

The notions in tasawwuf such as sacrificing from "kamalāt fuyuzāt", extra optional/nafawil for the good or benefit of others are considered as a better virtue than keeping and collecting them. Therefore, some of the late or contemporary approaches of scholars criticized some mutasawwifun, other scholars that they were stingy in their richness of spiritual endeavors while many were in spiritual draught and dead conditions due to lack or absence of the true imān. These scholars for their time implicitly disagreed respectfully to some of the mutasaawifin due to not sharing the basic spiritual help for the vital need of others so that they don't die.

One can realize in the consequence of the ayahs in this Sûrah, the first ayah underlines the necessary required state and the most valuable asset of imān as mentioned[83] آمَنَ الرَّسُولُ بِمَا أُنزِلَ إِلَيْهِ مِن رَّبِّهِ وَالْمُؤْمِنُونَ كُلٌّ آمَنَ بِاللَّهِ وَمَلَائِكَتِهِ وَكُتُبِهِ وَرُسُلِهِ لَا نُفَرِّقُ بَيْنَ أَحَدٍ مِّن رُّسُلِهِ وَقَالُوا سَمِعْنَا وَأَطَعْنَا غُفْرَانَكَ رَبَّنَا وَإِلَيْكَ الْمَصِيرُ {البقرة/285}. The starting of this ayah underlines this with the word آمَنَ.

The following ayah requires maintaining this most valuable asset imān for the person in this life and afterlife through the challenges, engagements, and interactions of taklîf as mentioned لَا يُكَلِّفُ اللَّهُ نَفْسًا إِلَّا وُسْعَهَا لَهَا مَا كَسَبَتْ وَعَلَيْهَا مَا اكْتَسَبَتْ رَبَّنَا لَا تُؤَاخِذْنَا إِن نَّسِينَا أَوْ أَخْطَأْنَا رَبَّنَا وَلَا تَحْمِلْ عَلَيْنَا إِصْرًا كَمَا حَمَلْتَهُ عَلَى الَّذِينَ مِن قَبْلِنَا رَبَّنَا وَلَا تُحَمِّلْنَا مَا لَا طَاقَةَ لَنَا بِهِ وَاعْفُ عَنَّا وَاغْفِرْ لَنَا وَارْحَمْنَا أَنتَ مَوْلَانَا فَانصُرْنَا عَلَى الْقَوْمِ الْكَافِرِينَ {البقرة/286}[84]. The starting of this ayah underlines this with the word لَا يُكَلِّفُ.

Yet, in this battle between imān, as the most valuable asset of the person, and taklîf, as the opponent of imān in the realities of life, one should not trust oneself, but ask help, forgiveness, refuge and easiness from Allah ﷻ as mentioned وَاعْفُ عَنَّا وَاغْفِرْ لَنَا وَارْحَمْنَا أَنتَ مَوْلَانَا فَانصُرْنَا عَلَى الْقَوْمِ الْكَافِرِينَ {البقرة/286}.

The ones who have these humble attitudes inshAllah will win and be respecful with the Rahmah, Fadl, Mercy and Grace of Allah ﷻ even though they may not have much knowledge.

The ones who may have these arrogant attitudes may lose, (May Allah ﷻ protect us) even though they could have the highest knowledge with the Adl (Justice) of Allah ﷻ.

Allahumma Ja'alna min allazina tabi'u sabila Rasuluk ﷺ, Amìn.

أللهم جَعَلْنَا مِن أَلَّذِينَ التِّبعوا سبيل رَسُولِك ﷺ، آمين

---

83. The Messenger has believed in what was revealed to him from his Lord, and [so have] the believers. All of them have believed in Allah and His angels and His books and His messengers, [saying], "We make no distinction between any of His messengers." And they say, "We hear and we obey. [We seek] Your forgiveness, our Lord, and to You is the [final] destination."

84. Allah does not charge a soul except [with that within] its capacity. It will have [the consequence of] what [good] it has gained, and it will bear [the consequence of] what [evil] it has earned. "Our Lord, do not impose blame upon us if we have forgotten or erred. Our Lord, and lay not upon us a burden like that which You laid upon those before us. Our Lord, and burden us not with that which we have no ability to bear. And pardon us; and forgive us; and have mercy upon us. You are our protector, so give us victory over the disbelieving people."

Juz 10

Sûrah 8

[46]

وَأَطِيعُواْ اللَّه وَرَسُولَهُ وَلاَ تَنَازَعُواْ فَتَفْشَلُواْ وَتَذْهَبَ رِيحُكُمْ وَاصْبِرُواْ إِنَّ اللَّه مَعَ الصَّابِرِينَ
{الأنفال/46}85

وَلَقَدْ صَدَقَكُمُ اللَّهُ وَعْدَهُ إِذْ تَحُسُّونَهُم بِإِذْنِهِ حَتَّى إِذَا فَشِلْتُمْ وَتَنَازَعْتُمْ فِي الأَمْرِ وَعَصَيْتُم مِّن بَعْدِ مَا أَرَاكُم مَّا تُحِبُّونَ مِنكُم مَّن يُرِيدُ الدُّنْيَا وَمِنكُم مَّن يُرِيدُ الآخِرَةَ ثُمَّ صَرَفَكُمْ عَنْهُمْ لِيَبْتَلِيَكُمْ وَلَقَدْ عَفَا عَنكُمْ وَاللَّهُ ذُو فَضْلٍ عَلَى الْمُؤْمِنِينَ {آل عمران/152}86

يَا أَيُّهَا الَّذِينَ آمَنُواْ أَطِيعُواْ اللَّه وَأَطِيعُواْ الرَّسُولَ وَأُوْلِي الأَمْرِ مِنكُمْ فَإِن تَنَازَعْتُمْ فِي شَيْءٍ فَرُدُّوهُ إِلَى اللَّهِ وَالرَّسُولِ إِن كُنتُمْ تُؤْمِنُونَ بِاللَّهِ وَالْيَوْمِ الآخِرِ ذَلِكَ خَيْرٌ وَأَحْسَنُ تَأْوِيلاً {النساء/59}87

Conflicts and Disputes in Families

The word تَنَازَعُواْ in the above ayahs can indicate the possible reality of conflicts among people.

It is a reality as humans that we have conflicts. Conflicts can arise due to difference of opinions. These differences can be as simple as choosing a color for painting a wall, or when to travel as a family, or if the family should travel or not, or who to travel with them and others.

In all these engagements, there can be dominant characters who may not change their opinions and emphasize their point and their choice to be executed.

---

85. And obey Allah and His Messenger, and do not dispute and [thus] lose courage and [then] your strength would depart; And obey Allah and His Messenger, and do not dispute and [thus] lose courage and [then] your strength would depart; and be patient. Indeed, Allah is with the patient.

86. And Allah had certainly fulfilled His promise to you when you were killing the enemy by His permission until [the time] when you lost courage and fell to disputing about the order [given by the Prophet] and disobeyed after He had shown you that which you love. Among you are some who desire this world, and among you are some who desire the Hereafter. Then he turned you back from them [defeated] that He might test you. And He has already forgiven you, and Allah is the possessor of bounty for the believers.

87. O you who have believed, obey Allah and obey the Messenger and those in authority among you. And if you disagree over anything, refer it to Allah and the Messenger, if you should believe in Allah and the Last Day. That is the best [way] and best in result.

Yet, in a family, a person who does not promote conflict with the intention of pleasing Allah ﷻ can be raised to a higher status with the Grace, Fadl and Rahmah of Allah ﷻ.

Yet, this is not easy. A person who may have another opinion for the matter and approached by the dominant characters forcing their opinion on him or her can require a lot of patience and wisdom, hikmah to handle these different and complex cases. The expression وَاصْبِرُوا إِنَّ اللّٰهَ مَعَ الصَّابِرِينَ can indicate and emphasize this critical and very difficult trait and quality of patience. Yet, the ones who are patient are the winners most of the time.

Conflicts and Disputes in Groups

One should realize that conflicts promoting disorder in group movements can also lead to chaos and dissolution of these group movements.

Especially, when people do things for the sake of Allah ﷻ and to please Allah ﷻ, people can use their mind, emotions and religious teachings to justify their point.

Yet, sometimes, in all these justifications and discussions, a person may not be aware that he or she is acting as a member of group.

Group or jam'ah dynamics require working as a team, embodying solidarity, and complementary functions together. Allah ﷻ is pleased with the people who come together and work in a discipline and structure to please Allah ﷻ. The structure of lines in five daily prayers in the masājid remind the person this group work presented to the Rabbul Alamin.

Yet, when the individual egos take the stance of using unending arguments to prove about the superiority of their opinions, then they can promote alienation and isolation from the group movement for themselves and for others. Although this person's choice could be right, yet one should not insist if other opinions are also acceptable.

Individual genius efforts are less valuable and profitable in the works of the dīn than collective mediocre or ordinary efforts.

May Allah ﷻ make us not one of the people generating conflicts but make us embody the character of Rasulullah ﷺ with gentleness, harmony and kindness promoting unity for the sake of Allah ﷻ, Amīn.

Juz 11

Sûrah 10- Yunûs

[96-101]

إِنَّ الَّذِينَ حَقَّتْ عَلَيْهِمْ كَلِمَتُ رَبِّكَ لاَ يُؤْمِنُونَ {يونس/96}[88]

وَلَوْ جَاءتْهُمْ كُلُّ آيَةٍ حَتَّى يَرَوُاْ الْعَذَابَ الأَلِيمَ {يونس/97}

فَلَوْلاَ كَانَتْ قَرْيَةٌ آمَنَتْ فَنَفَعَهَا إِيمَانُهَا إِلاَّ قَوْمَ يُونُسَ لَمَّا آمَنُواْ كَشَفْنَا عَنْهُمْ عَذَابَ الْخِزْيِ فِي الْحَيَاةَ الدُّنْيَا وَمَتَّعْنَاهُمْ إِلَى حِينٍ {يونس/98} وَلَوْ شَاء رَبُّكَ لآمَنَ مَن فِي الأَرْضِ كُلُّهُمْ جَمِيعًا أَفَأَنتَ تُكْرِهُ النَّاسَ حَتَّى يَكُونُواْ مُؤْمِنِينَ {يونس/99} وَمَا كَانَ لِنَفْسٍ أَن تُؤْمِنَ إِلاَّ بِإِذْنِ اللّهِ وَيَجْعَلُ الرِّجْسَ عَلَى الَّذِينَ لاَ يَعْقِلُونَ {يونس/100} قُلِ انظُرُواْ مَاذَا فِي السَّمَاوَاتِ وَالأَرْضِ وَمَا تُغْنِي الآيَاتُ وَالنُّذُرُ عَن قَوْمٍ لاَّ يُؤْمِنُونَ {يونس/101}

The Deadly Efforts of Fame as an Intrinsic Human Desire

One should take heed from the case of Qarûn as mentioned[89] وَأَصْبَحَ الَّذِينَ تَمَنَّوْا مَكَانَهُ بِالأَمْسِ يَقُولُونَ وَيْكَأَنَّ اللَّهَ يَبْسُطُ الرِّزْقَ لِمَن يَشَاء مِنْ عِبَادِهِ وَيَقْدِرُ لَوْلَا أَن مَّنَّ اللَّهُ عَلَيْنَا لَخَسَفَ بِنَا وَيْكَأَنَّهُ لَا يُفْلِحُ الْكَافِرُونَ {القصص/82}

Our spiritual diseases require that even if we do things for the sake of Allah, we want to receive some type of recognition from people. This is such a deadly and foxy disease that is similar to a black ant walking in a dark room, invisible and soundless as mentioned by Rasulullah ﷺ [16] (#715). This is called riya. One cannot sometimes know their own motivation in the good-looking engagements of religion until one dies. May Allah ﷻ protect us. The hadith of three religious and generous

---

88. Indeed, those upon whom the word of your Lord has come into effect will not believe, Even if every sign should come to them, until they see the painful punishment. Then has there not been a [single] city that believed so its faith benefited it except the people of Jonah? When they believed, We removed from them the punishment of disgrace in worldly life and gave them enjoyment for a time. And had your Lord willed, those on earth would have believed—all of them entirely. Then, [O Muhammad], would you compel the people in order that they become believers? And it is not for a soul to believe except by permission of Allah, and He will place defilement upon those who will not use reason. Say, "Observe what is in the heavens and earth." But of no avail will be signs or warners to a people who do not believe
89. And those who had wished for his position the previous day began to say, "Oh, how Allah extends provision to whom He wills of His servants and restricts it! If not that Allah had conferred favor on us, He would have caused it to swallow us. Oh, how the disbelievers do not succeed!"

people thrown into the hellfire can emphasize and allude this deadly, and sneaky concept of riya [3] [17]. They did not recognize this disease in themselves until they die and meet with Allah ﷻ. At the end, their all efforts were nullified.

The Similarity and Difference Between Yunus alayhi salam, Nuh alayhi salam, Ibrahim alayhi salam and Rasulullah ﷺ

When we review the efforts of Yunus (عليه السلام) and Rasulullah ﷺ, one of the emergent similarities between two prophets asm is the case of their zeal and overarching desire for people's hidayah. This can be due to the heavy responsibility of prophethood of Allah ﷻ placed on them. This can be also due the zeal for the hidayah of others as part of sharing.

In this effort of concern for others, one of the very unique and differentiating factor of Rasulullah ﷺ is that Rasulullah ﷺ makes all the efforts to save people from Jahannam either by attending their funeral until the clear instructions [14][90] being revealed to him ﷺ not to do otherwise. He ﷺ tried to make the rulings as easy as possible even sometimes easier than its apparent meanings as presented in the Qurãn. There are many examples of this.

Muwafaqqat Omar (رضى الله عنه) actually mostly emphasizes the mercy of Rasulullah ﷺ that may seem sometimes opposite the apparent meanings of the Qurãn in the initial nuzûl of the ayahs. Then, this becomes complete with the methodology of nasikh and mansuqh. The existence of nasikh and mansuqh and muwaffaqat Omar ra all prove that the Qurãn is not the word of Rasulullah ﷺ and he ﷺ was being corrected.

On the other hand, Allah ﷻ emphasizes the overarching mercy of Rasulullah ﷺ for all humanity and creation with all these cases as mentioned[91] لَقَدْ جَاءَكُمْ رَسُولٌ مِّنْ أَنفُسِكُمْ عَزِيزٌ عَلَيْهِ مَا عَنِتُّمْ حَرِيصٌ عَلَيْكُم بِالْمُؤْمِنِينَ وَمَا أَرْسَلْنَاكَ إِلَّا رَحْمَةً لِّلْعَالَمِينَ {107/الأنبياء} and[92] رَءُوفٌ رَّحِيمٌ {128/التوبة}.

Yet, one of the things that can be observed in the case of Rasulullah ﷺ, although Rasulullah ﷺ implements mercy, easiness and gentleness with all the creation, he ﷺ still maintains the highest level of adab with

---

90. Volume 2, Book 23, Number 447
91. There has certainly come to you a Messenger from among yourselves. Grievous to him is what you suffer; [he is] concerned over you and to the believers is kind and merciful.
92. And We have not sent you, [O Muhammad], except as a mercy to the worlds.

Allah 🙵. When the order is clear and explicit from Allah 🙵, Rasulullah 🙼 implements the order without any hesitation. In other words, if there are people who are designated to be the people of Jahannam, Rasulullah 🙼 maintains the same highest Adab with Allah 🙵. In other words, the zeal of Rasulullah 🙼 does not pass the Rida of Allah 🙵 in none of the cases.

One should review the cases of Yunus(عليه السلام) as mentioned in tafasir leaving his as people in the utmost zeal of hidayah and responsibility of messengership towards his people.

One should review the case of Nuh (عليه السلام) as mentioned in the Qurān for his zeal about his son's hidayah, then there is an explicit order comes in the Qurān about this case. He, Nuh (عليه السلام), makes istigfar, and tawbah for any possibility of zallah, as not overpassing the Rida of Allah 🙵 for the Divine Decree for them.

One should review the case of Ibrahim (عليه السلام), and his istigfar for his father. Allah 🙵 clarifies his situation in the Qurān so that there is no misunderstanding that Khalilullah as does not overpass the Rida of Allah 🙵 about the Divine Decree.

Sharing: Zeal for the Hidayah of Others

One should really view dawah, and tabligh as part of the zeal of sharing but not being stingy. If a person has a bread and food, if the neighbor is hungry, then it is required to share with them according to almost all religions.

The spiritual hunger can lead spiritual dead and physical dead through the cases of psychology, committing suicide, depression, anxiety, meaningless, and purposelessness.

In this sense efforts of tag words such missionary work, proselytization, or conversion can imply club or a fan related membership effort for being saved or punished.

Yet, the true and genuine approach of prophets is the notion of the zeal and desire of sharing what they have the most valuable for them to share with others. If others accept for their use in their needs, that is great. If they don't, then there is no force or compulsion.

This concept is **Not** a soothing way of presenting the religion or religious teachings in a disguised forms or "entering from the back door". Today, when people suffer from increased depression, anxiety, or stress especially with the recent pandemic of COVID 19, the most secular state departments such as New York sends a suggested resource center called Headspace promoting mindfulness studies. When one reviews the immediate website of this program and this initiative , the founder, an American Buddhist Monk after his religious and spiritual journey in Buddhism, comes back to people to "share" these teachings with others to benefit them. This motivation is exactly explained by this monk in his initiative of this program.

I think there is nothing wrong for any person to share what they have with the intention of benefitting others but not withholding and being stingy with knowledge, wealth and spirituality. In this regard, if this initiative is acceptable resulting from Buddhism, I think it is fair to look other ones, such as Abrahamic religions and Islãm in the search of if or how can people have relevance to benefit themselves with these teachings of spirituality, self-relevance, and the core of La ilaha illa Allah. This core really focuses on the person to discharge of all anxieties, worries, and stresses with Dhikr in Islãm and mantras in Buddhism.

Satisfaction after Sharing

When people see a hungry person, and if the person feeds them, there is a pleasure of satisfaction and happiness. Allah ﷻ immediately rewards the person with this personal satisfaction. Yet, the real reward comes with the pleasure of Allah ﷻ in the akhirah.

When a person sees a spiritual hungry person, if the person offers them what they have, there is a pleasure of satisfaction and happiness, when the helper witnesses the helped coming out of her or his troubles of chaotic, dark, pessimistic, depressive, anxious and stressful perspectives and views without imãn.

Today, in American and most part of the world, people really don't have much need for physical help with the social support systems. People today have much more advanced institutions, organizations, policies, and guidelines for a complex and comfortable live style of luxury.

Yet, the internal-spiritual heart parts of these individuals can be spiritually bleeding due to absence of a fulfilling, complete and perfect religion.

In social theories of functionalism, it is recognized and acknowledged that religion is a need [18].

Updating Yourself but Not Leaving What You Have

It is difficult to leave the identities. Therefore, the Qurān does not tell people of the book to leave what they have but advises them to maintain their true religious identity of being Christian and Jew by updating themselves, by removing the errors and bugs in the existing theologies introduced over the centuries deviating from their original teachings.

This is one of the mistakes and fears people see as a hindrance against change. When the Qurān engages the readers of ahlu-kitab, Christians and Jews, there is a given value for them in the Qurān and in the practices of Rasulullah ﷺ.

In this regard, what is really expected from an unbiased, objective, and open-minded Christian or Jew is that to realize this value that is given by Allah ﷻ for them in the Qurān and in the practices of Rasulullah ﷺ.

After this recognition, they can really look into if the Qurān really wants them to leave everything that they have. The answer is NO.

The Qurān and Rasulullah ﷺ constantly, repetitively, clearly and explicitly teaches a very genuine style as:

1. Recognize their high and elect status with Allah ﷻ as they knew the scriptures and teachings from Allah ﷻ before Muslims.
2. Inform them that the Qurān is another book of Allah ﷻ similar to Gospel and Torah.
3. Inform them to recognize the changed/altered theologies related with the creed in their scriptures.
4. Invite them to consider updating themselves from these bugs/errors as introduced into their books, Gospel and Torah by humans over centuries due to different reasons.
5. Inform that to recognize the changed/altered rituals related with the rituals in their practices over time and invite them to consider updating themselves.

Muslims also have diseases of not understanding, practicing and accordingly appreciating what type of valuable asset they have.

May Allah ﷻ forgive us and give us guidance, Amìn

Allahumma Salli ala Sayyidina Muhammad ﷺ, al-Mustafa ﷺ, al-Habìb ﷺ.

اللهم صلى على سيدنا محمد ﷺ، المصطفى ﷺ،الحبيب ﷺ

Juz 12

[18]

وَجَاؤُوا عَلَى قَمِيصِهِ بِدَمٍ كَذِبٍ قَالَ بَلْ سَوَّلَتْ لَكُمْ أَنفُسُكُمْ أَمْرًا فَصَبْرٌ جَمِيلٌ وَاللَّهُ الْمُسْتَعَانُ عَلَى مَا تَصِفُونَ {يوسف/18}⁹³

When we analyze the above ayah it really highlights a lot of critical approaches in our relations with humans, children, friends, and others.

Not Exposing Faults and Still Maintaining the Level of Respect

When Yaqûb (عليه السلام) knew and actually understood his sons plot against Yûsuf as, he did not expose their faults.

As we live in life, we make mistakes. Others make mistake. The suggested way is not to expose their mistakes by confronting them on their faces. Sometimes our egos or nafs want to slash back by exposing the mistakes of others. Shaytān tries to legitimize this slashing back with the so-called virtue of correcting the person. Yet, each slash back or confrontation or exposing one's mistakes to their faces generally cause resentment on the people and makes them as enemies.

There can be some few awliyaullah that they may not be bothered when their mistakes are exposed and told to them. Yet, our principles are based on general notions of nafs-ammarah that most of us initially hold.

Sometimes, when others make mistakes, we try to be more tolerant about implementing this rule of not exposing their mistakes. Yet, when they are family members and children that one can have some type of authority on them, then Shaytān seem to give us another so-called legitimization point of exposing their mistakes with the virtue of correcting them because they are the person's children.

Yet, regardless, nafs-ammara in its very raw form does not accept any criticism even if it comes from parents or teachers who did so much for the person.

---

93. And they brought upon his shirt false blood. [Jacob] said, "Rather, your souls have enticed you to something, so patience is most fitting. And Allah is the one sought for help against that which you describe."

One of the worst and lowest and raw form of this nafs-ammara is when there are teachings that come from Allah ﷻ, yet the person tries to find excuses and although Allah ﷻ did so much for the person giving life from non-existence to existence as mentioned[94] كَيْفَ تَكْفُرُونَ بِاللَّهِ وَكُنْتُمْ أَمْوَاتاً فَأَحْيَاكُمْ ثُمَّ يُمِيتُكُمْ ثُمَّ يُحْيِيكُمْ ثُمَّ إِلَيْهِ تُرْجَعُونَ {البقرة/28}.

In that sense, Allah ﷻ mentions in the Qurān very logical, vivid and relevant descriptions and examples referred as ayahs or signs. Yet, some of the people still maintains this attitude of belligerent and rude attitude of blaming religion, God and without any adab using a language of enemy as mentioned[95] أَوَلَمْ يَرَ الْإِنسَانُ أَنَّا خَلَقْنَاهُ مِن نُطْفَةٍ فَإِذَا هُوَ خَصِيمٌ مُبِينٌ {يس/77}.

Today's increasing books and shameless titles of these books give this problematic extreme of these belligerent attitudes. I don't want to mention these titles in order to not bring the feelings of disgust on the heart and mind. May Allah ﷻ protect us, Amìn.

Yet, Allah ﷻ uses very gentle language for them to realize these notions of imān called gratitude in order to avoid ingratitude referred as kufr in the Qurān. Yet, our raw egos still maintain this issue of not accepting. This is mentioned in the Qurān with the word Jahūlā as:

إِنَّا عَرَضْنَا الْأَمَانَةَ عَلَى السَّمَاوَاتِ وَالْأَرْضِ وَالْجِبَالِ فَأَبَيْنَ أَن يَحْمِلْنَهَا وَأَشْفَقْنَ مِنْهَا وَحَمَلَهَا الْإِنسَانُ إِنَّهُ كَانَ ظَلُومًا جَهُولًا {الأحزاب/72}[96]

Yet the uslûb of a'fw is required with the people of Jahūlā as mentioned[97] خُذِ الْعَفْوَ وَأْمُرْ بِالْعُرْفِ وَأَعْرِضْ عَنِ الْجَاهِلِينَ {الأعراف/199}

In the reality of free will of a person with our raw and unfiltered egos, we tend to reject our mistakes initially. Yet, at our times of self-reflection with some spiritual openings with the Fadl and Grace of Allah ﷻ and/or sometimes due to some very painful tests or trials, we realize these mistakes. After this realization if we accept it humbly and now,

---

94. How can you disbelieve in Allah when you were lifeless and He brought you to life; then He will cause you to die, then He will bring you [back] to life, and then to Him you will be returned.

95. Does man not consider that We created him from a [mere] sperm-drop—then at once he is a clear adversary?

96. Indeed, we offered the Trust to the heavens and the earth and the mountains, and they declined to bear it and feared it; but man [undertook to] bear it. Indeed, he was unjust and ignorant.

97. Take what is given freely, enjoin what is good, and turn away from the ignorant.

change our selves, then this is called as guidance, or Hidayah. This is with the Fadl and Rahmah of Allah ﷻ.

If we realize these mistakes but we don't accept it, this is still not a guidance, or Hidayah.

Realization of a mistake requires acceptance of it. Acceptance of it requires a change in the person. This is called Hidayah.

The sign of a hidayah is a positive change in the person. If there is no sign, one may not talk about the existence of Hidayah, acceptance of one's mistakes or even realization of these mistakes.

May Allah ﷻ give us Hidayah, Amìn.

Ihdina siratal mustaqim, siratalllazine ana'amta alayhim gayrul magdubi alayhim wa la Dallin, Amìn.

Not Getting Angry

In all these engagements, one of the critical stances is that a human faculty needs a constant control, balance and modulation. This faculty is called gadab or anger. In the above case, from an Islamic Jurisprudence or legal rulings, if the father, Yaqub(عليه السلام) got angry and accordingly acted, then there is no impermissibility for this stance as a parent.

Yet, although anger is a motivating factor to keep the person balanced against the injustices, oppressions, and evil as mentioned by Imam Ghazali [12] (رحمه الله), one's attitude or uslûb should be modulated without not fully executing the force and momentum related with anger.

One should admit that humans are really in a very difficult stance of having complex emotional and spiritual faculties in constant self-struggle (jihad) to please Allah ﷻ but not displease Allah ﷻ by not acting unjust.

Sometimes a feeling or a deriving emotion needs to be modulated and balanced with another. All the feelings and emotions have a purpose and they all have complementary roles balancing each other. Absence of one can reflect a diseased and imbalanced person.

Yet, the modulation and balance of all these feelings and emotions are critical for an ideal human being. Rasulullah ﷺ was the prime example of implementing this modulation and balance for all of these emotions and feelings.

Uslub of External Dress as a'fw and Embodiment of Internal dress as Sabr

When we analyze the ayah[98] خُذِ الْعَفْوَ وَأْمُرْ بِالْعُرْفِ وَأَعْرِضْ عَنِ الْجَاهِلِينَ {الأعراف/199} and فَصَبْرٌ جَمِيلٌ in this ayah, one can realize two important related notions.

In this case, there are two critical terms one is patience in its specific and internal context and the other is a'fw of uslûb as the practice in its general or outer context.

When a person is under the effect of different conflicting emotions, then patience is the term that is used to indicate suppressing and modulating the emotions that can lead to extremities and imbalance of the emotions.

When a person gets angry, in this case Yaqub (عليه السلام) with his children, he can very well discipline his children and execute sanctions on them. Today's secular law enforcements and even the religious legal rulings of implementing justice require an immediate action of discipline and execution of sanctions against the mischiefs and evil. This is the rule of Justice being applied to everyone.

Yet, in their higher level, one can prefer a'fw and patience as mentioned[99] يَا أَيُّهَا الَّذِينَ آمَنُوا إِنَّ مِنْ أَزْوَاجِكُمْ وَأَوْلَادِكُمْ عَدُوًّا لَّكُمْ فَاحْذَرُوهُمْ وَإِن تَعْفُوا وَتَصْفَحُوا وَتَغْفِرُوا فَإِنَّ اللَّهَ غَفُورٌ رَّحِيمٌ {التغابن/41}

This stance is only to please Allah ﷻ and ask help from Allah ﷻ. Then, with this approach one can see and realize the Divine pleasure of Allah ﷻ in this life and afterlife. One can realize again this critical stance of uslûb in the above ayah, although executing the discipline can be a form of justice, yet, one can acquire enemies as mentioned يَا أَيُّهَا الَّذِينَ آمَنُوا إِنَّ مِنْ أَزْوَاجِكُمْ وَأَوْلَادِكُمْ عَدُوًّا لَّكُمْ.

When the person confront people with their mistakes even if they are family members such as spouses and children, they can become enemies. Yet, the non-confrontation way of moving on with patience is a higher level minimizing the problems and conflicts as mentioned وَإِن تَعْفُوا وَتَصْفَحُوا وَتَغْفِرُوا.

---

98. Take what is given freely, enjoin what is good, and turn away from the ignorant.
99. O you who have believed, indeed, among your wives and your children are enemies to you, so beware of them. But if you pardon and overlook and forgive—then indeed, Allah is Forgiving and Merciful.

Although our general emotions burn and push us internally and spiritually to execute discipline measures, yet prophetic uslûb handles this overarching emotions with the balance of patience for a better result. This better result can come with a lot of blessings and openings from Allah ﷻ in this life and afterlife.

When we analyze the Qurãn, this modeled uslûb can be sometimes called taqwa. Yet, this uslûb is the one that is higher than applying the apparent justice. This uslûb is the one that opens a lot of doors and openings for the person in this life and after life although adapting this uslûb requires patience and sacrifice as an internal dress and sometimes or most of the time silence on the tongue and smile on the face as an external dress of uslûb as mentioned with the word a'fw as:

وَإِن طَلَّقْتُمُوهُنَّ مِن قَبْلِ أَن تَمَسُّوهُنَّ وَقَدْ فَرَضْتُمْ لَهُنَّ فَرِيضَةً فَنِصْفُ مَا فَرَضْتُمْ إِلَّا أَن يَعْفُونَ أَوْ يَعْفُوَ الَّذِي بِيَدِهِ عُقْدَةُ النِّكَاحِ وَأَن تَعْفُواْ أَقْرَبُ لِلتَّقْوَى وَلَا تَنسَوُاْ الْفَضْلَ بَيْنَكُمْ إِنَّ اللَّهَ بِمَا تَعْمَلُونَ بَصِيرٌ {البقرة/237}[100]

لَا يُحِبُّ اللَّهُ الْجَهْرَ بِالسُّوءِ مِنَ الْقَوْلِ إِلَّا مَن ظُلِمَ وَكَانَ اللَّهُ سَمِيعًا عَلِيمًا {النساء/148}[101] إِن تُبْدُواْ خَيْرًا أَوْ تُخْفُوهُ أَوْ تَعْفُواْ عَن سُوءٍ فَإِنَّ اللَّهَ كَانَ عَفُوًّا قَدِيرًا {النساء/149}

Allah ﷻ mentions in these above set of ayahs first the option of legal rulings related with Justice. Then, Allah ﷻ mentions a higher level with a'fw.

May Allah ﷻ give us this stance of a'fw, Amìn.

Witnessing a Nation due to this Patience

In this case of Yaqub (عليه السلام), one can witness a whole nation coming from one person. This can be, Allahu A'lam, due to patience of Yaqub (عليه السلام) in the case of Yusuf (عليه السلام). If Yaqub (عليه السلام) acted with anger, the brothers can be all scattered around, and the family could have been all dispersed and separated.

---

100. And if you divorce them before you have touched them and you have already specified for them an obligation, then [give] half of what you specified—unless they forego the right or the one in whose hand is the marriage contract foregoes it. And to forego it is nearer to righteousness. And do not forget graciousness between you. Indeed Allah, of whatever you do, is Seeing.
101. Allah does not like the public mention of evil except by one who has been wronged. And ever is Allah Hearing and Knowing. If [instead] you show [some] good or conceal it or pardon an offense—indeed, Allah is ever Pardoning and Competent.

Yet, the incident of the patience of Yaqub (عليه السلام) could have led a nation with the Barakah and Fadl of Allah ﷻ, what we call today is the Bānū Isrā'īl (children of Israel), Yaqub (as).

Therefore, in each great difficulty taken for the sake of Allah ﷻ, Allah ﷻ can give great openings in this life and afterlife, SubhanAllah! This reality is mentioned as[102] وَرَفَعْنَا لَكَ ذِكْرَكَ {الشرح/4} فَإِنَّ مَعَ الْعُسْرِ يُسْرًا {الشرح/5} إِنَّ مَعَ الْعُسْرِ يُسْرًا {الشرح/6}

Asking Help and the Pleasure only from Allah ﷻ

In all these engagements, the primary source of help and taking refuge is Allah ﷻ. The primary reason and motivation are to please Allah ﷻ.

One should not to embody patience due to pleasing others or due to the expectations of receiving great openings from Allah ﷻ. One should only embody patience to please Allah ﷻ. A'fw and forgiving others for their mistakes leads to the pleasure of Allah ﷻ. The implementation of a'fw and forgiveness of others requires patience.

When a person embodies this dress and quality of a'fw with patience, then Allah ﷻ is pleased with this person and forgives this person as mentioned[103] وَلاَ يَأْتَلِ أُوْلُوا الْفَضْلِ مِنكُمْ وَالسَّعَةِ أَن يُؤْتُوا أُوْلِي الْقُرْبَى وَالْمَسَاكِينَ وَالْمُهَاجِرِينَ فِي سَبِيلِ اللّهِ وَلْيَعْفُوا وَلْيَصْفَحُوا أَلَا تُحِبُّونَ أَن يَغْفِرَ اللّهُ لَكُمْ وَاللّهُ غَفُورٌ رَّحِيمٌ {النور/22}

Allahumma Ja'alna minhum, Amìn

أللهم جَعَلَنَا مِنهُم ، آمين

Reflection of the Divine Names and Attributes on Humans

One should remember that we are trying to please Allah ﷻ by being a tiny reflection of the Divine Names and Attributes of Allah ﷻ on the earth. When we hear he hadith about "Allah ﷻ created humans in the Divine image", this can be due to human's reflection of some of the Divine Names and Attributes of Allah ﷻ as the khalifah on the earth.

---

102. And raised high for you your repute. For indeed, with hardship [will be] ease. Ineed, with hardship [will be] ease.

103. And let not those of virtue among you and wealth swear not to give [aid] to their relatives and the needy and the emigrants for the cause of Allah, and let them pardon and overlook. Would you not like that Allah should forgive you? And Allah is Forgiving and Merciful.

In the case of a'fw, Allah ﷻ has the Absolute and Perfect and Full Attribute and Name of al-A'fuw. When we analyze the Qurān, Allah ﷻ mentions this Divine Name and Attribute as[104]

وَهُوَ الَّذِي يَقْبَلُ التَّوْبَةَ عَنْ عِبَادِهِ وَيَعْفُو عَنِ السَّيِّئَاتِ وَيَعْلَمُ مَا تَفْعَلُونَ {الشورى/25}

وَمَا أَصَابَكُم مِّن مُّصِيبَةٍ فَبِمَا كَسَبَتْ أَيْدِيكُمْ وَيَعْفُو عَن كَثِيرٍ {الشورى/30}[105]

الَّذِينَ يُظَاهِرُونَ مِنكُم مِّن نِّسَائِهِم مَّا هُنَّ أُمَّهَاتِهِمْ إِنْ أُمَّهَاتُهُمْ إِلَّا اللَّائِي وَلَدْنَهُمْ وَإِنَّهُمْ لَيَقُولُونَ مُنكَرًا مِّنَ الْقَوْلِ وَزُورًا وَإِنَّ اللَّهَ لَعَفُوٌّ غَفُورٌ {المجادلة/2}[106]

Most and all of the time we deserve justice of punishment, yet Allah ﷻ forgives us. When we face evil, May Allah ﷻ protect us, it is due our renderings of kasb. When we most of the time don't see the outcome of the evils that we engage, that is due to Name and Attribute of Allah ﷻ as al-A'fw.

Allahumma inna asaluka afwa wal afiyata fidunya walakhirah, Amìn.

أللهم اِنِّى أسألُك العَفوَ وَالعَافِيَة فِي الدُنيَا وَالآخِرَة ، آمين

Juz 13

Sûrah 13 -Al-Rā'd

[28]

الَّذِينَ آمَنُواْ وَتَطْمَئِنُّ قُلُوبُهُم بِذِكْرِ اللّهِ أَلاَ بِذِكْرِ اللّهِ تَطْمَئِنُّ الْقُلُوبُ {الرعد/28}[107]

When we analyze the above ayah around the disturbances of the heart, one of the interesting words that come is أَلاَ before بِذِكْرِ اللّهِ.

---

104. And it is He who accepts repentance from his servants and pardons misdeeds, and He knows what you do.
105. And it is He who accepts repentance from his servants and pardons misdeeds, and He knows what you do.
106. Those who pronounce thihar among you [to separate] from their wives—they are not [consequently] their mothers. Their mothers are none but those who gave birth to them. And indeed, they are saying an objectionable statement and a falsehood. But indeed, Allah is Pardoning and Forgiving.
107. Those who have believed and whose hearts are assured by the remembrance of Allah. Unquestionably, by the remembrance of Allah hearts are assured."

In another ayah the same word is used in[108] أَلَا إِنَّ أَوْلِيَاء اللّهِ لَا خَوْفٌ عَلَيْهِمْ
وَلَا هُمْ يَحْزَنُونَ {يونس/62}.

When we combine these two ayahs around the word أَلَا, one can possibly deduce that one of the major disturbances of the heart occur around fear as mentioned with the word خَوْفٌ. Fear can entail the feelings of worry, anxiety, stress, concern, nervousness, agitation, discomfort, and unease.

This disturbed state of the heart with fear is at times very difficult to calm down. Yet, the word أَلَا indicates that the only way to calm down the heart with any disturbances and especially the father of all disturbances, fear is with Dhikrullah. The people who have this habit of practice are called awliyaullah أَوْلِيَاء اللّهِ.

In this regard, teachings of Buddhism or Hinduism can engage the person with mindfulness and mediation to calm the heart and mind. Although there can be a partial calming down of the heart, one can ask as can this practice also be appreciated by Allah ﷻ? Can this people also be awliyaullah? The other is no. Because awliyaullah gains the both benefit of calming the heart and the benefit of pleasure of Allah ﷻ in this life and afterlife through the Dhikrullah.

Dhikrullah is defined with the pre-conditions of imān and implementing the teaching of the Qurān and Sunnah as the requirements of the imān referred as taqwa. This is mentioned[109] الَّذِينَ آمَنُواْ وَكَانُواْ يَتَّقُونَ {يونس/63}.

Then compared to Buddhism or others seeking immediate peace, Dhikrullah and awliyaullah have both peace and happiness in this life and afterlife as mentioned[110] لَهُمُ الْبُشْرَى فِي الْحَيَاةِ الدُّنْيَا وَفِي الآخِرَةِ لاَ تَبْدِيلَ لِكَلِمَاتِ
اللّهِ ذَلِكَ هُوَ الْفَوْزُ الْعَظِيمُ {يونس/64}.

In this sense, there can be some indications with the phrase لاَ تَبْدِيلَ لِكَلِمَاتِ اللّهِ that the current practices of Buddhism, mediation or yoga can be some remnants of the true religion of Allah ﷻ that was sent before. Yet, as people could have possibly changed the core changings of these religions, only some benefits could have remained in them and main

---

108. Unquestionably, [for] the allies of Allah there will be no fear concerning them, nor will they grieve
109. Those who believed and were fearing Allah
110. For them are good tidings in the worldly life and in the Hereafter. No change is there in the words of Allah. That is what is the great attainment.

benefit through the true tawhid and imān may not be there, Allahu A'lam.

Then, one can review the consequences of the ayahs as[111] أَلَا إِنَّ أَوْلِيَاءَ اللَّهِ لَا خَوْفٌ عَلَيْهِمْ وَلَا هُمْ يَحْزَنُونَ {يونس/62} الَّذِينَ آمَنُوا وَكَانُوا يَتَّقُونَ {يونس/63} لَهُمُ الْبُشْرَى فِي الْحَيَاةِ الدُّنْيَا وَفِي الْآخِرَةِ لَا تَبْدِيلَ لِكَلِمَاتِ اللَّهِ ذَٰلِكَ هُوَ الْفَوْزُ الْعَظِيمُ {يونس/64}.

Juz 15

Sûrah 18 – al-Kahf

[19-20]

وَكَذَٰلِكَ بَعَثْنَاهُمْ لِيَتَسَاءَلُوا بَيْنَهُمْ قَالَ قَائِلٌ مِّنْهُمْ كَمْ لَبِثْتُمْ قَالُوا لَبِثْنَا يَوْمًا أَوْ بَعْضَ يَوْمٍ قَالُوا رَبُّكُمْ أَعْلَمُ بِمَا لَبِثْتُمْ فَابْعَثُوا أَحَدَكُم بِوَرِقِكُمْ هَٰذِهِ إِلَى الْمَدِينَةِ فَلْيَنظُرْ أَيُّهَا أَزْكَى طَعَامًا فَلْيَأْتِكُم بِرِزْقٍ مِّنْهُ وَلْيَتَلَطَّفْ وَلَا يُشْعِرَنَّ بِكُمْ أَحَدًا {الكهف/19}[112] إِنَّهُمْ إِن يَظْهَرُوا عَلَيْكُمْ يَرْجُمُوكُمْ أَوْ يُعِيدُوكُمْ فِي مِلَّتِهِمْ وَلَن تُفْلِحُوا إِذًا أَبَدًا {الكهف/20}

Izhār and Ikhfā in Social Life

When we analyze the above ayahs, one can realize the realities of izhar and ikhfa as a term in tajwid. Izhar is the notion of being explicit, public and open. Ikhfa is the notion of hiding. Mixing the places of izhar and ikhfa is considered as an error in the rules of tajwid.

Similarly, as mentioned in the above ayah, some of the realities of social life living with others, making dawah or tabligh to others and being an activist against the injustices as instructed by Allah ﷻ may require the similar notions of izhar and ikhfa. When a person maintains the publicity, openness, and explicitness, where the notions of implicitness

---

111. Unquestionably, [for] the allies of Allah there will be no fear concerning them, nor will they grieve Those who believed and were fearing Allah For them are good tidings in the worldly life and in the Hereafter. No change is there in the words of Allah. That is what is the great attainment.
112. And similarly, We awakened them that they might question one another. Said a speaker from among them, "How long have you remained [here]?" They said, "We have remained a day or part of a day." They said, "Your Lord is most knowing of how long you remained. So send one of you with this silver coin of yours to the city and let him look to which is the best of food and bring you provision from it and let him be cautious. And let no one be aware of you. Indeed, if they come to know of you, they will stone you or return you to their religion. And never would you succeed, then—ever."

is required, then this can be a mistake as mentioned[113] إِنَّهُمْ إِن يَظْهَرُوا عَلَيْكُمْ يَرْجُمُوكُمْ أَوْ يُعِيدُوكُمْ فِي مِلَّتِهِمْ وَلَن تُفْلِحُوا إِذًا أَبَدًا {الكهف/20}.

There can be the opposite case of this as well. The person or people of Allah ﷻ is expected to make izhar, publicity or explicitness but they do ikhfa hiding, and implicitness, then this can be a mistake as well.

The notions of izhar and ikhfa are realities of successful tabligh and dawah for the sake of Allah ﷻ and even in the rules of social etiquettes, or interactions referred as mubasharāt. Rasulullah ﷺ implemented this approach as mentioned[114] إِلاَّ تَنصُرُوهُ فَقَدْ نَصَرَهُ اللّهُ إِذْ أَخْرَجَهُ الَّذِينَ كَفَرُواْ ثَانِيَ اثْنَيْنِ إِذْ هُمَا فِي الْغَارِ إِذْ يَقُولُ لِصَاحِبِهِ لاَ تَحْزَنْ إِنَّ اللّهَ مَعَنَا فَأَنزَلَ اللّهُ سَكِينَتَهُ عَلَيْهِ وَأَيَّدَهُ بِجُنُودٍ لَّمْ تَرَوْهَا وَجَعَلَ كَلِمَةَ الَّذِينَ كَفَرُواْ السُّفْلَى وَكَلِمَةُ اللّهِ هِيَ الْعُلْيَا وَاللّهُ عَزِيزٌ حَكِيمٌ {التوبة/40}

The initial followers of Isa (as) as the disciples had this approach as well as mentioned[115] يَا أَيُّهَا الَّذِينَ آمَنُوا كُونوا أَنصَارَ اللَّهِ كَمَا قَالَ عِيسَى ابْنُ مَرْيَمَ لِلْحَوَارِيِّينَ مَنْ أَنصَارِي إِلَى اللَّهِ قَالَ الْحَوَارِيُّونَ نَحْنُ أَنصَارُ اللَّهِ فَآمَنَت طَّائِفَةٌ مِّن بَنِي إِسْرَائِيلَ وَكَفَرَت طَّائِفَةٌ فَأَيَّدْنَا الَّذِينَ آمَنُوا عَلَى عَدُوِّهِمْ فَأَصْبَحُوا ظَاهِرِينَ {الصف/14}.

Yet, in the above cases of ikhfa, the notion of fear is normal. There are people who want to oppress, kill and terminate the people due to their beliefs. Yet, the people of high status like Rasulullah ﷺ even may not bear the notions of fear at the times of ikhfa as mentioned إِذْ يَقُولُ لِصَاحِبِهِ لاَ تَحْزَنْ إِنَّ اللّهَ مَعَنَا.

One can also remember the fearless approach of Ibrahim (as) in the case of izhar challenging the norms of the beliefs of his society as a single person. Yet, Allah ﷻ saved him. Similarly, Musa (عليه السلام), mumin-ali Firawn challenged the norms of the beliefs of Firawn, Allah ﷻ saved them.

It seems that, Allahu A'lam, Allah ﷻ knows the best, depending the ahwāl of the person, if he wants to meet with Allah ﷻ as soon as possible and becomes shahīd, Allah ﷻ can grant them this level too as

---

113. Indeed, if they come to know of you, they will stone you or return you to their religion. And never would you succeed, then—ever."
114. If you do not aid the Prophet—Allah has already aided him when those who disbelieved had driven him out [of Makkah] as one of two, when they were in the cave and he said to his companion, "Do not grieve; indeed Allah is with us." And Allah sent down his tranquillity upon him and supported him with angels you did not see and made the word of those who disbelieved the lowest, while the word of Allah—that is the highest. And Allah is Exalted in Might and Wise.
115. O you who have believed, be supporters of Allah, as when Jesus, the son of Mary, said to the disciples, "Who are my supporters for Allah?" The disciples said, "We are supporters of Allah." And a faction of the Children of Israel believed and a faction disbelieved. So We supported those who believed against their enemy, and they became dominant.

in the case of Najjar (رحمه الله) as mentioned in Sûrah Yasin. The below ayah can indicate especially a type of a desire on his part to be a shahid Allahu A'lam, Allah ﷺ knows the best,[116] قِيلَ ادْخُلِ الْجَنَّةَ قَالَ يَا لَيْتَ قَوْمِي يَعْلَمُونَ {يس/26} بِمَا غَفَرَ لِي رَبِّي وَجَعَلَنِي مِنَ الْمُكْرَمِينَ {يس/27}.

At another perspective, the people who are shahid are not considered death. Therefore, there is still protection on them as an another perspective.

Juz 18

Sûrah 24 -Al-Nûr

[36-38]

فِي بُيُوتٍ أَذِنَ اللَّهُ أَن تُرْفَعَ وَيُذْكَرَ فِيهَا اسْمُهُ يُسَبِّحُ لَهُ فِيهَا بِالْغُدُوِّ وَالْآصَالِ {النور/36}[117]

رِجَالٌ لَّا تُلْهِيهِمْ تِجَارَةٌ وَلَا بَيْعٌ عَن ذِكْرِ اللَّهِ وَإِقَامِ الصَّلَاةِ وَإِيتَاءِ الزَّكَاةِ يَخَافُونَ يَوْمًا تَتَقَلَّبُ فِيهِ الْقُلُوبُ وَالْأَبْصَارُ {النور/37} لِيَجْزِيَهُمُ اللَّهُ أَحْسَنَ مَا عَمِلُوا وَيَزِيدَهُم مِّن فَضْلِهِ وَاللَّهُ يَرْزُقُ مَن يَشَاءُ بِغَيْرِ حِسَابٍ {النور/38}

It is important to make dua to Allah ﷺ to be in the category of رِجَالٌ لَّا تُلْهِيهِمْ تِجَارَةٌ وَلَا بَيْعٌ عَن ذِكْرِ اللَّهِ. In our popular culture of an expression as "the real man" can best fit for the translation for the رِجَالٌ in this ayah.

The Qurãn has very charming and appealing feature to connect everyone to Allah ﷺ with a Sûrah, an ayah or even with a word or sound in the Qurãn. This ayah is one of the popular ayahs for lot of Muslims try to emulate and struggle to be in the content category of this ayah.

When we analyze the expression رِجَالٌ لَّا تُلْهِيهِمْ تِجَارَةٌ وَلَا بَيْعٌ عَن ذِكْرِ اللَّهِ from its opposite, we can understand that there can be many people who are prevented to make the dhikr of Allah ﷺ due to their engagements of the world. Yet, this barrier of prevention is not in accordance with what Allah ﷺ is pleased with for the real purpose of the person's existence

---

116. It was said, "Enter Paradise." He said, "I wish my people could know Of how my Lord has forgiven me and placed me among the honored."

117. [Such niches are] in mosques which Allah has ordered to be raised and that His name be mentioned therein; exalting Him within them in the morning and the evenings [Are] men whom neither commerce nor sale distracts from the remembrance of Allah and performance of prayer and giving of zakah. They fear a Day in which the hearts and eyes will [fearfully] turn about—That Allah may reward them [according to] the best of what they did and increase them from His bounty. And Allah gives provision to whom He wills without account.

in life. Yet, we may hear a lot of Muslims trying to justify their busy schedule to normalize and justify their prevention to do the dhikr and remembrance of Allah ﷻ.

The suggested way of life is having engagement of the world, yet this engagement should not prevent us to remember Allah ﷻ as mentioned[118] رِجَالٌ لَّا تُلْهِيهِمْ تِجَارَةٌ وَلَا بَيْعٌ عَن ذِكْرِ اللَّهِ وَإِقَامِ الصَّلَاةِ وَإِيتَاءِ الزَّكَاةِ يَخَافُونَ يَوْمًا تَتَقَلَّبُ فِيهِ الْقُلُوبُ وَالْأَبْصَارُ {النور/37}.

Some of the indications of these above ayahs can be the people of Allah ﷻ as a group instead of an individual or self as indicated with the plural form in رِجَالٌ and بُيُوتٍ. In that sense, the group work with others on the path of Allah ﷻ is critical.

Yet, when we analyze both words رِجَالٌ and بُيُوتٍ, both can indicate not necessarily big groups but small and even, a few people as well.

Therefore, in group associations of doing a good and ethical work, sometimes we are swayed with the quantities and numbers. Yet, Allah ﷻ values our actions through the quality of ikhlas, sincerity. Yet, one of the expected actions that we are expected to do is with others in the form of dhikr, salah, charity in the form of helping others as mentioned ذِكْرِ اللَّهِ وَإِقَامِ الصَّلَاةِ وَإِيتَاءِ الزَّكَاةِ.

It is difficult combine both our worldly needs and dhikr of Allah ﷻ due to our tendencies to imbibe imbalance. Yet, these people of zuhd are the people who Allah ﷻ can give them much and increase the bounties on them both in this world and afterlife as mentioned[119] لِيَجْزِيَهُمُ اللَّهُ أَحْسَنَ مَا عَمِلُوا وَيَزِيدَهُم مِّن فَضْلِهِ وَاللَّهُ يَرْزُقُ مَن يَشَاءُ بِغَيْرِ حِسَابٍ {النور/38}

Allahumma Ja'alna min allazina لِيَجْزِيَهُمُ اللَّهُ أَحْسَنَ مَا عَمِلُوا وَيَزِيدَهُم مِّن فَضْلِهِ

Amìn.

أللهم جَعَلَنَا مِن الذين لِيَجْزِيَهُمُ اللَّهُ أَحْسَنَ مَا عَمِلُوا وَيَزِيدَهُم مِّن فَضْلِهِ آمين

---

118. [Are] men whom neither commerce nor sale distracts from the remembrance of Allah and performance of prayer and giving of zakah. They fear a Day in which the hearts and eyes will [fearfully] turn about

119. That Allah may reward them [according to] the best of what they did and increase them from His bounty. And Allah gives provision to whom He wills without account.

Juz 19

Sûrah 26 -al-Shua'rã

[4]

إِن نَّشَأْ نُنَزِّلْ عَلَيْهِم مِّن السَّمَاء آيَةً فَظَلَّتْ أَعْنَاقُهُمْ لَهَا خَاضِعِينَ {الشعراء/4}120

Free Will Reality

When we analyze and review the ayahs of the Qurãn, one can clearly realize the notion of the reality of the free will as granted by Allah ﷻ to each human being and Jinn.

A person sometimes may be misled and mix the two issues of free will and the forced notion of people believing in Allah ﷻ with true tawhid.

The Qurãn clearly and explicitly addresses this critical notion with the above ayah of the main focus as well as other ayahs as:[121]

وَلَوْ شَاء رَبُّكَ لآمَنَ مَن فِي الأَرْضِ كُلُّهُمْ جَمِيعًا أَفَأَنتَ تُكْرِهُ النَّاسَ حَتَّى يَكُونُواْ مُؤْمِنِينَ {يونس/99}

لاَ إِكْرَاهَ فِي الدِّينِ قَد تَّبَيَّنَ الرُّشْدُ مِنَ الْغَيِّ فَمَنْ يَكْفُرْ بِالطَّاغُوتِ وَيُؤْمِن بِاللّهِ فَقَدِ اسْتَمْسَكَ بِالْعُرْوَةِ الْوُثْقَىَ لاَ انفِصَامَ لَهَا وَاللّهُ سَمِيعٌ عَلِيمٌ {البقرة/256}122

Especially, the expression in the above ayah emphasizes the required practice of not forcing people to believe that is going to interfere with their free will as mentioned لاَ إِكْرَاهَ فِي الدِّينِ.

At another level, the expression أَفَأَنتَ تُكْرِهُ النَّاسَ حَتَّى يَكُونُواْ مُؤْمِنِينَ can express a judgment free approach in the engagements of dawah, tabligh and other inter-faith.

---

120. If We willed, We could send down to them from the sky a sign for which their necks would remain humbled.
121. And had your Lord willed, those on earth would have believed—all of them entirely. Then, [O Muhammad], would you compel the people in order that they become believers?
122. There shall be no compulsion in [acceptance of] the religion. The right course has become clear from the wrong. So whoever disbelieves in Taghut and believes in Allah has grasped the most trustworthy handhold with no break in it. And Allah is Hearing and Knowing.

Yes, when we analyze لاَ إِكْرَاهَ فِي الدِّينِ and لآمَنَ مَن فِي الأَرْضِ كُلُّهُمْ جَمِيعًا, one should realize the reality of the free will as given to each human and Jinn for their choices in their life.

Especially, if the most critical choice in one's life is imān versus kufr, then even in this critical choice, Allah ﷻ mentions that لاَ إِكْرَاهَ فِي الدِّينِ.

Value of Forced vs By Will Choice

One should realize why free will is so critical. A deliberate and determined choice executed by free will has a value. A forced choice does not have any value.

A choice executed with free will shows the person as a being. A forced choice does not make the person different than an unanimated object due to its stagnant disposition of no choice.

In today's educational terms, the concept of "relevancy' in learning and teaching are the efforts of trying to show the student or a person on the path the value of engagement by free-will choice. In other words, if a person may find the knowledge relevant, then he or she can engage naturally due to its benefits as executed by free-will compared to the boring perspectives of learning and classical methods.

Free will requires personal and self-related critical thinking. Free will requires taking the responsibility on oneself in the journey of life regardless of good or bad decisions. Free will makes every person similar to a separate complex universe in their execution of the free will in the constant life engagements changing with pain, suffering, happiness, deaths, divorces, marriages, births, accomplishments and losses.

Yet, all these free will engagements can make the person ask a bigger and more important questions of:

- ▶ Why I am doing what I am doing?
- ▶ What is the purpose of all these engagements?
- ▶ How can I stabilize myself with my emotions trying to be always content, calm and happy but not affected with pain?
- ▶ What is going to happen to me after death?

Iman

The answer of all these questions is *Intention. The absolute and true intention is imān.*

Free will requires intention. The true and absolute intention is imān.

Imān is the life perspective of the self finding, realizing, and accepting all of the favors of Allah ﷻ *on the person with free will and by choice.*

Yet, in this journey of the self, Allah ﷻ does not force. The person realizes all these favors of existence, life, being a human being with free will, health, family, food, air, habitat of living, earth, sky, trees, house, dress and others.

The *realization* of all them is the first ayah of the Qurān and called[123] بِسْمِ اللهِ الرَّحْمَنِ الرَّحِيمِ {الفاتحة/1}. Therefore, this ayah is repeated in the beginning of all the Sūrahs of the Qurān.

The *acceptance* of this realization is called imān as[124] الْحَمْدُ لِلّٰهِ رَبِّ الْعَالَمِينَ {الفاتحة/2} الرَّحْمنِ الرَّحِيمِ {الفاتحة/3} مَلِكِ يَوْمِ الدِّينِ {الفاتحة/4}. Therefore, endless nim'ahs of Allah ﷻ are constantly repeated and reminded the person in the Qurān.

Imān is acceptance of this realization. This acceptance is gratitude. Imān is gratitude.

The *highest level of gratitude* is the embodiment of the Divine phrase الْحَمْدُ لِلّٰهِ.

This true gratitude is only for Allah ﷻ. Therefore, the word hamd is only used for Allah ﷻ.

The rest of the ayahs as الْحَمْدُ لِلّٰهِ رَبِّ الْعَالَمِينَ {الفاتحة/2} الرَّحْمنِ الرَّحِيمِ {الفاتحة/3} مَلِكِ يَوْمِ الدِّينِ {الفاتحة/4} are all different critical Names and Attributes of Allah ﷻ reminding the person immediately why the person needs to have gratitude leading to imān.

---

123. In the name of Allah, the Entirely Merciful, the Especially Merciful.
124. [All] praise is [due] to Allah, Lord of the worlds—The Entirely Merciful, the Especially Merciful, Sovereign of the Day of Recompense.

(Modern) Slaves vs A'bd of Allah ﷻ

One can ask a very basic question: why do people today much seem to appreciate their affiliations with their employer such as corporations or institutions compared to their affiliations with Allah ﷻ? Although Allah ﷻ fulfills their need daily in the basic needs of habitat, air, existence and food coming from the ground, water or all others, why this is the case?

When a person is surrounded with hindrances preventing and blurring his or her execution of the free will, then a person can be called *slave or modern slave*. Physical slavery is human-bounded. Mindful and heartful-spiritual slavery is self-bounded. The spiritual slavery is worse than physical slavery.

In that regard, one can remember the embodiment of our role model Yusuf (عليه السلام). He (as) prefers the freedom from spiritual slavery over the freedom of physical slavery. He prefers to be in prison, in physical slavery conditions compared to the spiritual slavery of luxury conditions of physical freedom. This is mentioned as[125] قَالَ رَبِّ السِّجْنُ أَحَبُّ إِلَيَّ مِمَّا يَدْعُونَنِي إِلَيْهِ وَإِلاَّ تَصْرِفْ عَنِّي كَيْدَهُنَّ أَصْبُ إِلَيْهِنَّ وَأَكُن مِّنَ الْجَاهِلِينَ {يوسف/33}.

Today, there are billions who are in comfortable physical conditions. Yet, they have the chains of spiritual slavery. There may be only few who are in physical slavery conditions of difficult life. Yet, they may have the spiritual freedom by being only A'bd of Allah ﷻ.

Therefore, the real freedom referred as hurriyah is not much dependent on the propagandist notions of freedom.

The real freedom is the self-realization of oneself that one can really execute their free will.

Honorary or Lowly Position of Free Will Investment

In this regard, Allah ﷻ creates and gives us life and all other parts of life in the respected reality of free will as mentioned[126] وَلَقَدْ كَرَّمْنَا بَنِي آدَمَ وَحَمَلْنَاهُمْ فِي الْبَرِّ وَالْبَحْرِ وَرَزَقْنَاهُم مِّنَ الطَّيِّبَاتِ وَفَضَّلْنَاهُمْ عَلَى كَثِيرٍ مِّمَّنْ خَلَقْنَا تَفْضِيلاً {الإسراء/70}.

---

125. He said, "My Lord, prison is more to my liking than that to which they invite me. And if You do not avert from me their plan, I might incline toward them and [thus] be of the ignorant."
126. And We have certainly honored the children of Adam and carried them on the land and sea and provided for them of the good things and preferred them over much of what We have created, with [definite] preference.

In other words, Allah ﷻ increases our respect and honor beyond all the creation and existence with free will as mentioned وَلَقَدْ كَرَّمْنَا بَنِي آدَمَ and وَفَضَّلْنَاهُمْ عَلَى كَثِيرٍ مِّمَّنْ خَلَقْنَا تَفْضِيلاً.

Yet, every honorary position has some expectations and responsibilities. The ones who don't fulfill these expectations and responsibilities can be referred as Jahûl, ignorant, and Zâlim, oppressor. This is mentioned as[127] إِنَّا عَرَضْنَا الْأَمَانَةَ عَلَى السَّمَاوَاتِ وَالْأَرْضِ وَالْجِبَالِ فَأَبَيْنَ أَن يَحْمِلْنَهَا وَأَشْفَقْنَ مِنْهَا وَحَمَلَهَا الْإِنسَانُ إِنَّهُ كَانَ ظَلُومًا جَهُولًا {الأحزاب/72}.

In this regard, this free will was an amanah, a loan, a responsibility, and an advanced credit. Some did not want to take any advanced credit such as the skies, earth, or the mountains as mentioned إِنَّا عَرَضْنَا الْأَمَانَةَ عَلَى السَّمَاوَاتِ وَالْأَرْضِ وَالْجِبَالِ فَأَبَيْنَ أَن يَحْمِلْنَهَا وَأَشْفَقْنَ مِنْهَا. They possibly said "We are happy by being abd of Allah ﷻ in our natural disposition of creation. We don't know if we are going to make more profit with this advanced credit of free-will with investments to please Allah ﷻ more. Or, we are going to lose all this advanced credit of free-will in wrong and false risky gambling and displease Allah ﷻ." They preferred to be in so called unanimated positions as described by humans. Yet, these unanimated entities of sky, universe, earth or others constantly make dhikr, tasbîh and remember Allah ﷻ with natural and loving dispositions of gratitude.

Yet, humans are opportunistic and rushing as mentioned[128] وَيَدْعُ الْإِنسَانُ بِالشَّرِّ دُعَاءَهُ بِالْخَيْرِ وَكَانَ الْإِنسَانُ عَجُولًا {الإسراء/11}. This attitude of "jumping in" without the proper and correct intention make the ones lose this opportunity and advanced investment. They become as مِنْهَا وَحَمَلَهَا الْإِنسَانُ إِنَّهُ كَانَ ظَلُومًا جَهُولٌ. They were ignorant because they did not make the proper intention of pleasing Allah ﷻ. They were oppressor because they oppressed their own selves by losing their advanced credit in wrong investments. A peak example of this is Shaytân from the Jinn. Shaytân was allowed to be with the angels with the permission of Allah ﷻ. Yet, he lost by investing his free will in a wrong place.

Therefore, some of the humans or Jinn called kâfir will desire to be in the positions of these unanimated beings mentioned above in the Judgment Day or Accountability of Advance Payments of Free Will

---

127. Indeed, we offered the Trust to the heavens and the earth and the mountains, and they declined to bear it and feared it; but man [undertook to] bear it. Indeed, he was unjust and ignorant.

128. There the believers were tested and shaken with a severe shaking.

due to not investing their advanced credit of free will in life. This is mentioned as[129] وَيَقُولُ الْكَافِرُ يَا لَيْتَنِي كُنتُ تُرَابًا {40/النبأ}.

Yet, there are the few ones who had the proper intention with the Fadl and Karam, and Grace of Allah ﷻ used their advanced investment in such a way that they pleased Allah ﷻ with their intention and action in life as mentioned وَلَقَدْ كَرَّمْنَا بَنِي آدَمَ وَحَمَلْنَاهُمْ فِي الْبَرِّ وَالْبَحْرِ.

The pleasure of Allah ﷻ with these individuals was in such a way that they even exceeded angels and become so close to Allah ﷻ. A peak example of this was Rasulullah ﷺ.

One can realize that in both ayahs of the same word حَمَلْنَاهُمْ is used to indicate the advanced credit payment of free-will as[130]

وَلَقَدْ كَرَّمْنَا بَنِي آدَمَ وَحَمَلْنَاهُمْ فِي الْبَرِّ وَالْبَحْرِ وَرَزَقْنَاهُم مِّنَ الطَّيِّبَاتِ وَفَضَّلْنَاهُمْ عَلَى كَثِيرٍ مِّمَّنْ خَلَقْنَا تَفْضِيلاً {70/الإسراء}

إِنَّا عَرَضْنَا الْأَمَانَةَ عَلَى السَّمَاوَاتِ وَالْأَرْضِ وَالْجِبَالِ فَأَبَيْنَ أَن يَحْمِلْنَهَا وَأَشْفَقْنَ مِنْهَا وَحَمَلَهَا الْإِنسَانُ إِنَّهُ كَانَ ظَلُومًا جَهُولًا {72/الأحزاب}[131]

The above first ayah indicates people who follow the path of Rasulullah ﷺ with their free will as mentioned with the word وَلَقَدْ كَرَّمْنَا بَنِي آدَمَ. Rasulullah ﷺ is the peak and lead of this path.

The above second ayah indicates people who follow the path of Shaytān with their free will as mentioned with the expression الْإِنسَانُ إِنَّهُ كَانَ ظَلُومًا جَهُولٌ. Shaytān is the peak and lead of this path.

In both above ayahs, the usage of the same word حَمَلْنَاهُمْ can indicate, the free will is given as an amanah to carry. In this carriage as mentioned with this word حَمَلْنَاهُمْ, there is an accountability. Hammāl is a carrier in Arabic.

---

129. Indeed, We have warned you of a near punishment on the Day when a man will observe what his hands have put forth and the disbeliever will say, "Oh, I wish that I were dust!"
130. And We have certainly honored the children of Adam and carried them on the land and sea and provided for them of the good things and preferred them over much of what We have created, with [definite] preference.
131. And whoever is blind in this [life] will be blind in the Hereafter and more astray in way.

Corporations & Institutions and Imãn, Free Will

After this honorary position given with free will by not fulfilling these responsibilities, the person makes him or herself traditional or modern slaves under entities, beings, and internal or external fears or emotions.

With all these dependencies on Allah ﷻ for the showering favors, such as existence, habitat, earth, life, nature, disease, microbes, health and others, Allah ﷻ still does not force the person to believe due to the humans' reality of free will.

On the other hand, our humanly generated or existent preferences make us follow all the guidelines, policies, orders, and commands of our employers, institutions, or corporations. The person has a fearful forced choice. Sometimes that has an immediate consequence such as losing one's job, not being promoted or others.

A true free will of expectancy of a person in their life span requires free execution of the decisions. Allah ﷻ makes the person exposed to different signs and ayahs from Allah ﷻ about the real dependency of each person to Allah ﷻ. Yet, the person decides for imãn and kufr with their free will. The decision and execution of imãn is with the decision of the person with the Fadl and Rahmah and Grace of Allah ﷻ. The decision and execution of kufr is with the decision of the person with the Just, Adl of Allah ﷻ.

In the first case of slavery or modern slavery, there may not be much appreciation by the corporation when the person is fired or retired.

In the second case, when the person realizes this full dependency in Allah ﷻ with their free-will, they knock the Divine Door. As soon as they knock the Door with imãn, they are so much welcomed that they adorn and become the 'abd of Allah ﷻ.

In this regard, being true 'abd of Allah ﷻ for humans and Jinn include the free will. In other words, one of the differentiation factors of humans and jinn being a'bd of Allah ﷻ compared to other beings, there is the free will execution of humans towards imãn with the Fadl, Grace and Rahmah of Allah ﷻ. In the latter case of other beings, they have the intrinsic position of 'abd of Allah ﷻ as mentioned[132] إِن كُلُّ مَن فِي السَّمَاوَاتِ وَالْأَرْضِ إِلَّا آتِي الرَّحْمَنِ عَبْدًا {مريم/93}. If the ones who don't understand their 'abd position to Allah ﷻ with their free will by being exposed to

---

132. There is no one in the heavens and earth but that he comes to the Most Merciful as a servant.

millions of signs and ayah, then they would know this in clear reality in the afterlife. May Allah ﷻ make us realize for being the true 'abd of Allah ﷻ in this life, Amìn.

Islām

Once the person realizes all the favors of Allah ﷻ and accepts their full dependency on Allah ﷻ with their free will, then this called imān. This is indicated in[133] مَلِكِ {الفاتحة/3} الرَّحْمنِ الرَّحِيمِ {الفاتحة/2} الْحَمْدُ لِلّهِ رَبِّ الْعَالَمِينَ .يَوْمِ الدِّينِ {الفاتحة/4}

Showing the gratitude as being the 'abd of Allah ﷻ with gratitude, hamd, dhikr, salah, dua and other rituals then are called Islām. This indicated in[134] إِيَّاكَ نَعْبُدُ وإِيَّاكَ نَسْتَعِينُ {الفاتحة/5}. The core of Islām is five daily prayers as indicated in the fifth ayah of Sûrah Fatiha.

At the position of Islām, 'abd of Allah ﷻ as Abdullah only expresses his or her gratitude, tasbìh, hamd, dhikr, dependency internally and externally with ibadah only truly for Allah ﷻ as mentioned إِيَّاكَ نَعْبُدُ.

At the position of Islām, 'abd of Allah ﷻ as Abdullah asks all his or her needs truly from Allah ﷻ as mentioned وإِيَّاكَ نَسْتَعِينُ.

Then, being steadfast on the journey with imān and Islām is called ihsān. This is indicated in[135]

اهِدِنَا الصِّرَاطَ الْمُسْتَقِيمَ {الفاتحة/6} صِرَاطَ الَّذِينَ أَنْعَمْتَ عَلَيهِمْ غَيرِ الْمَغْضُوبِ عَلَيهِمْ وَلاَ الضَّالِّينَ {الفاتحة/7}

Ihsān: Loyalty-Sidq Versus Interest Based Relation

Ihsan requires true loyalty and sidq. Ihsan requires appreciating all the favors truly from only Allah ﷻ. If there are times, the favors seem to be less than before, then loyalty-sidq to Allah ﷻ requires still being grateful but not rendering in the problems of blames or theodicy.

---

133. [All] praise is [due] to Allah, Lord of the worlds—The Entirely Merciful, the Especially Merciful Sovereign of the Day of Recompense.
134. It is You we worship and You we ask for help.
135. Guide us to the straight path—The path of those upon whom You have bestowed favor, not of those who have evoked [Your] anger or of those who are astray.

Most of problems of ahlu-kitāb, Christians and Jews are due to the issues of theodicy and blaming God due to absence of loyalty, sidq and ihsān.

Corporations, institutions and entities establish structure and order on interest-based relations. Once the corporation does not pay the employee, then the strikes start, and people leave the corporation.

This increased expectation of interest-based relations in corporate world affecting one's relationship with God in Western societies increase and normalize the issues of theodicy especially among the followers of Christians and Jews. Unfortunately, this is one of side effect teachings of corporate world on religions. Everything is based on **Immediate** benefits and interests. If there is no payment, no one can wait and be patient, the employees leave, and they go on strike.

In almost all religions, patience and loyalty are virtues. Especially in Abrahamic religions, Allah ﷻ can give the person some evil-seeming incidents, to reveal the reality of characters. In these incidents, some become stronger and some become weaker.

In this regard, once one starts on the journey of imān and Islām, ihsan is the safety valve to ensure the person on the straight path with loyalty and sidq. Absence of ihsan can generate people of magdubi alayhim and dāllin. This is indicated as[136] {الفاتحة/6} اهدِنَا الصِّرَاطَ المُسْتَقِيمَ

صِرَاطَ الَّذِينَ أَنعَمتَ عَلَيهِمْ غَيرِ المَغضُوبِ عَلَيهِمْ وَلاَ الضَّالِّينَ {الفاتحة/7}

May Allah ﷻ protect us from being magdubi alayhim and dāllin and keep us on ihdina siratal mustaqim, siratal allazina an'amta alayhim Amìn.

Sûrah 27 -al-Naml

[19]

فَتَبَسَّمَ ضَاحِكًا مِّن قَوْلِهَا وَقَالَ رَبِّ أَوْزِعْنِي أَنْ أَشْكُرَ نِعْمَتَكَ الَّتِي أَنْعَمْتَ عَلَيَّ وَعَلَى
وَالِدَيَّ وَأَنْ أَعْمَلَ صَالِحًا تَرْضَاهُ وَأَدْخِلْنِي بِرَحْمَتِكَ فِي عِبَادِكَ الصَّالِحِينَ {النمل/19}[137]

---

136. Guide us to the straight path—The path of those upon whom You have bestowed favor, not of those who have evoked [Your] anger or of those who are astray.

137. So [Solomon] smiled, amused at her speech, and said, "My Lord, enable me to be grateful for Your favor which You have bestowed upon me and upon my parents and to do righteousness of which You approve. And admit me by Your mercy into [the ranks of] Your righteous servants."

Math Equation & Istinbat

When analyze the above ayah with[138] وَوَصَّيْنَا الْإِنْسَانَ بِوَالِدَيْهِ إِحْسَانًا حَمَلَتْهُ أُمُّهُ كُرْهًا وَوَضَعَتْهُ كُرْهًا وَحَمْلُهُ وَفِصَالُهُ ثَلَاثُونَ شَهْرًا حَتَّى إِذَا بَلَغَ أَشُدَّهُ وَبَلَغَ أَرْبَعِينَ سَنَةً قَالَ رَبِّ أَوْزِعْنِي أَنْ أَشْكُرَ نِعْمَتَكَ الَّتِي أَنْعَمْتَ عَلَيَّ وَعَلَى وَالِدَيَّ وَأَنْ أَعْمَلَ صَالِحًا تَرْضَاهُ وَأَصْلِحْ لِي فِي ذُرِّيَّتِي إِنِّي تُبْتُ إِلَيْكَ وَإِنِّي مِنَ الْمُسْلِمِينَ {الأحقاف/15}, we realize some derivations similar to solving a math equation, SubhanAllah!

If anyone looks and reviews a math equation with variables, for example x and y for example,

x+y=5

3x+y =40

One can realize there are some similarities. Then, once the person solves the problem for the values of x and y, then he or she gets so much pleasure although the designer of the problem knows the answer. Yet, the solver of the problem engages oneself and gets pleasure after an effort or struggle he solves the problem.

In social sciences, this derivation can be called critical thinking, and analysis. In tafsir of the Qurān, this is called istinbat, deriving the meanings from the ocean of the Qurān, SubhanAllah!

When we compare two similar expressions in the below ayahs, one can realize some perspectives:[139]

قَالَ رَبِّ أَوْزِعْنِي أَنْ أَشْكُرَ نِعْمَتَكَ الَّتِي أَنْعَمْتَ عَلَيَّ وَعَلَى وَالِدَيَّ وَأَنْ أَعْمَلَ صَالِحًا تَرْضَاهُ وَأَدْخِلْنِي بِرَحْمَتِكَ فِي عِبَادِكَ الصَّالِحِينَ {النمل/19}

قَالَ رَبِّ أَوْزِعْنِي أَنْ أَشْكُرَ نِعْمَتَكَ الَّتِي أَنْعَمْتَ عَلَيَّ وَعَلَى وَالِدَيَّ وَأَنْ أَعْمَلَ صَالِحًا تَرْضَاهُ وَأَصْلِحْ لِي فِي ذُرِّيَّتِي إِنِّي تُبْتُ إِلَيْكَ وَإِنِّي مِنَ الْمُسْلِمِينَ {الأحقاف/15}[140]

---

138. And We have enjoined upon man, to his parents, good treatment. His mother carried him with hardship and gave birth to him with hardship, and his gestation and weaning [period] is thirty months. [He grows] until, when he reaches maturity and reaches [the age of] forty years, he says, "My Lord, enable me to be grateful for Your favor which You have bestowed upon me and upon my parents and to work righteousness of which You will approve and make righteous for me my offspring. Indeed, I have repented to You, and indeed, I am of the Muslims."

139. So [Solomon] smiled, amused at her speech, and said, "My Lord, enable me to be grateful for Your favor which You have bestowed upon me and upon my parents and to do righteousness of which You approve. And admit me by Your mercy into [the ranks of] Your righteous servants."

140. And We have enjoined upon man, to his parents, good treatment. His mother carried him with hardship and gave birth to him with hardship, and his gestation and weaning [period] is thirty months. [He grows] until, when he reaches maturity and reaches [the age of] forty years, he says, "My Lord, enable me to be grateful for Your favor which You have bestowed upon me and upon my parents and to work righteousness of which You will approve and make righteous for me my offspring. Indeed, I have repented to You, and indeed, I am of the Muslims."

Seeking Pleasure of Allah ﷻ in Amalu Salih

One of the critical important expressions to analyze is أَعْمَلَ صَالِحًا تَرْضَاهُ. Sometimes, we engage ourselves what we refer is as good amal or amalu salih, yet we don't know if Allah ﷻ is pleased with that or not.

In all the forms of good-looking engagements and actions, there is the possibility of pleasure of Allah ﷻ if they are done for the sake of Allah ﷻ solely with ikhlas, sincerity without any shirk and without any alternative motives. Therefore, one should not be safe, confident and secure in their good-looking engagements of amalu salih but ask Allah ﷻ to accept it and be pleased with us through this action or engagement.

At the end of the day, if we happen to enter Jannah and be among the salihìn, it is not due to the result of this amalu salih. It is due to Allah ﷻ 's Rahmah, Fadl and Grace as mentioned[141] وَأَدْخِلْنِي بِرَحْمَتِكَ فِي عِبَادِكَ الصَّالِحِينَ {النمل/19}

On the other hand, in all the forms of our good or evil-looking engagements and actions, there is the possibility of displeasure of Allah ﷻ. Therefore, one should ask constantly forgiveness and make tawbah to Allah ﷻ as mentioned إِنِّي تُبْتُ إِلَيْكَ وَإِنِّي مِنَ الْمُسْلِمِينَ {الأحقاف/15}. One should constantly ask Allah ﷻ to distance us from the haram and makruhāt and give ikhlas in our good-looking actions.

Family Endowments: Waqf

When one analyzes above ayahs, one of the common parts is the mention of the parents. Parents are ni'mah for the child. The children show their gratitude by remembering them in their dua. The children also are expected to realize that all the nimahs that are given to them individually, and at a family level.

Having a chain of parents and children establishes an institution or waqf of sadaqa-I Jariya for amalu salih, good actions. This is one of the ways of continuation of sadaqa-i jariya of good actions as mentioned by Rasulullah [3] ﷺ[142].

---

141. So [Solomon] smiled, amused at her speech, and said, "My Lord, enable me to be grateful for Your favor which You have bestowed upon me and upon my parents and to do righteousness of which You approve. And admit me by Your mercy into [the ranks of] Your righteous servants."
142. Hadith # 1631

The methodology or usûl of this establishment can be through the visible and invisible chains or institutions of waqfs coming from the families, parents and offspring.

Ahlu-Bayt Family Endowment

In this regard, the primary sadaqa-I Jariya, waqf or institution is established by Rasulullah ﷺ through Ahlu-Bayt.

Ahlu Bayt is today's concept of family endowment as established by Rasulullah ﷺ. In this regard, Rasulullah ﷺ emphasized the chain for ahlu bayt for the continuous spiritual, knowledge and physical transfer of wealth from one generation to another. Ahlu bayt mostly has been in the action of the transfer of spiritual and knowledge wealth. They did not acquire much worldly affairs to gain physical wealth.

Family: Game or Institution?

Today's increasing Western families can depict families as a game that everyone is playing individually rather than a person being part of an institution. A family endowment institution is established only after the families and the members in the family can view the family as an institution but not as a game. In games, people attract fans. In institutions, people work together for a goal and purpose. When the institution gains, everyone is happy. When the game is lost by that individual, then everyone is happy. Everything is based on competition. Physical, financial and mental powerful ones should win over the weak ones as part of the "scientific" extinction theory of evolution.

If today, one can realize some family endowment institutions, they are mostly established by religious people of different groups who understand family as an institution but not as a game [19].

In this regard, in the Qurān, one can realize the encouragement of establishment of the families through the establishment of tawhid, imān and amalu salih as the sunnatullah as mentioned[143]

وَاتَّبَعْتُ مِلَّةَ آبَائِي إِبْرَاهِيمَ وَإِسْحَقَ وَيَعْقُوبَ مَا كَانَ لَنَا أَن نُّشْرِكَ بِاللّهِ مِن شَيْءٍ ذَلِكَ مِن فَضْلِ اللّهِ عَلَيْنَا وَعَلَى النَّاسِ وَلَكِنَّ أَكْثَرَ النَّاسِ لاَ يَشْكُرُونَ {يوسف/38}

---

143. And I have followed the religion of my fathers, Abraham, Isaac and Jacob. And it was not for us to associate anything with Allah. That is from the favor of Allah upon us and upon the people, but most of the people are not grateful.

وَكَذَلِكَ يَجْتَبِيكَ رَبُّكَ وَيُعَلِّمُكَ مِن تَأْوِيلِ الأَحَادِيثِ وَيُتِمُّ نِعْمَتَهُ عَلَيْكَ وَعَلَى آلِ يَعْقُوبَ كَمَا
أَتَمَّهَا عَلَى أَبَوَيْكَ مِن قَبْلُ إِبْرَاهِيمَ وَإِسْحَقَ إِنَّ رَبَّكَ عَلِيمٌ حَكِيمٌ {يوسف/6}144

In this regard, one can realize that a common and unchanging
mission of the family endowment is iman with true tawhid in Allah ﷻ.
Its vision is the sunnatullah as brought by the prophets leading to amalu
salih as mentioned

وَوَصَّى بِهَا إِبْرَاهِيمُ بَنِيهِ وَيَعْقُوبُ يَا بَنِيَّ إِنَّ اللهَ اصْطَفَى لَكُمُ الدِّينَ فَلاَ تَمُوتُنَّ إِلاَّ وَأَنتُم
مُسْلِمُونَ {البقرة/132}145 أَمْ كُنتُمْ شُهَدَاء إِذْ حَضَرَ يَعْقُوبَ الْمَوْتُ إِذْ قَالَ لِبَنِيهِ مَا تَعْبُدُونَ
مِن بَعْدِي قَالُواْ نَعْبُدُ إِلَهَكَ وَإِلَهَ آبَائِكَ إِبْرَاهِيمَ وَإِسْمَاعِيلَ وَإِسْحَقَ إِلَهًا وَاحِدًا وَنَحْنُ لَهُ
مُسْلِمُونَ {البقرة/133}

In this regard, one should not understand the family endowments
as exclusivity or choosiness or privilege as mentioned146 قُلْ يَا أَيُّهَا الَّذِينَ هَادُوا
Family. إِن زَعَمْتُمْ أَنَّكُمْ أَوْلِيَاء لِلَّهِ مِن دُونِ النَّاسِ فَتَمَنَّوُا الْمَوْتَ إِن كُنتُمْ صَادِقِينَ {الجمعة/6}
endowments are means of encouragement of establishing the families
through the collective institution of imān, tawhid and amalu-salih.
Today, one can call this as a family endowment working towards good.

One can see that asking to Allah ﷻ to have an offspring is also
related with establishment of this sadaqa-I Jariya of family endowment
as mentioned147 وَإِنِّي خِفْتُ الْمَوَالِيَ مِن وَرَائِي وَكَانَتِ امْرَأَتِي عَاقِرًا فَهَبْ لِي مِن لَّدُنكَ
وَلِيًّا {مريم/5} يَرِثُنِي وَيَرِثُ مِنْ آلِ يَعْقُوبَ وَاجْعَلْهُ رَبِّ رَضِيًّا {مريم/6} يَا زَكَرِيَّا إِنَّا نُبَشِّرُكَ
بِغُلَامٍ اسْمُهُ يَحْيَى لَمْ نَجْعَل لَّهُ مِن قَبْلُ سَمِيًّا {مريم/7} قَالَ رَبِّ أَنَّى يَكُونُ لِي غُلَامٌ وَكَانَتِ
امْرَأَتِي عَاقِرًا وَقَدْ بَلَغْتُ مِنَ الْكِبَرِ عِتِيًّا {مريم/8}

---

144. And thus will your Lord choose you and teach you the interpretation of narratives and
complete His favor upon you and upon the family of Jacob, as He completed it upon your
fathers before, Abraham and Isaac. Indeed, your Lord is Knowing and Wise."

145. And Abraham instructed his sons [to do the same] and [so did] Jacob, [saying], "O
my sons, indeed Allah has chosen for you this religion, so do not die except while you are
Muslims." Or were you witnesses when death approached Jacob, when he said to his sons,
"What will you worship after me?" They said, "We will worship your God and the God of your
fathers, Abraham and Ishmael and Isaac—one God. And we are Muslims [in submission] to
Him."

146. Say, "O you who are Jews, if you claim that you are allies of Allah, excluding the [other]
people, then wish for death, if you should be truthful."

147. And indeed, I fear the successors after me, and my wife has been barren, so give me from
Yourself an heir Who will inherit me and inherit from the family of Jacob. And make him, my
Lord, pleasing [to You]." [He was told], "O Zechariah, indeed We give you good tidings of a boy
whose name will be John. We have not assigned to any before [this] name." He said, "My Lord,
how will I have a boy when my wife has been barren and I have reached extreme old age?"

One can encounter many of today's family endowment funds inspired by Christian and Judaism families from one generation another, especially with notions of continuation of silsila, or chain.

When we approach the good actions, amalu-salih as a family endowment or sadaqa-i jariya, one places value in everyone's effort in the family collectively helping each other to please Allah ﷻ.

In this regard, in the family, there is no or ineffective concepts of "I" or "my children" but there is the emphasis on "we" and "our children."

In this regard, today's Western individualistic approaches popularized with liberalism, feminism, current disciplines of social sciences such as sociology and psychology depicting structure and hierarchy as a negative means of abuse, can make the establishment of these family endowments more difficult.

Individuals in the families view divorce as the execution of the individual rights that can be done at any time on a personal preference. Therefore, the notions of "I" or "my children" in these types of families are some type of preparation for the possible execution of the right of divorce, and separation.

A parent, father or mother can constantly remind the child how much he or she did himself or herself for the child. He or she excludes the other spouse by not using a language of "we" while in communication with children in order to invest for the mental and emotional attachment of the child to this sole parent.

The parents especially can view this as a game to collect fans on their side when there is a dispute or divorce. In these types of families, it is very difficult to expect the altruistic types of unity, collectiveness, and harmony among the members. It is therefore very difficult to expect them to establish and work together for a family endowment funds with the intention of doing good to please Allah ﷻ collectively as a family. There can be some family endowment funds motivated to just a leave altruistic memory, or fame without much consideration of doing this altruism only to please Allah ﷻ.

Āl-Imran, Āl-Ibrahìm & Ahlu-Bayt Family Endowments

Yet, the current ayahs can emphasize this collectiveness as[148] قَالَ رَبِّ أَوْزِعْنِي أَنْ أَشْكُرَ نِعْمَتَكَ الَّتِي أَنْعَمْتَ عَلَيَّ وَعَلَى وَالِدَيَّ وَأَنْ أَعْمَلَ صَالِحًا تَرْضَاهُ وَأَدْخِلْنِي بِرَحْمَتِكَ فِي عِبَادِكَ الصَّالِحِينَ {النمل/19}

قَالَ رَبِّ أَوْزِعْنِي أَنْ أَشْكُرَ نِعْمَتَكَ الَّتِي أَنْعَمْتَ عَلَيَّ وَعَلَى وَالِدَيَّ وَأَنْ أَعْمَلَ صَالِحًا تَرْضَاهُ وَأَصْلِحْ لِي فِي ذُرِّيَّتِي إِنِّي تُبْتُ إِلَيْكَ وَإِنِّي مِنَ الْمُسْلِمِينَ {الأحقاف/15}[149]

Allah ﷻ mentions the collective achievement of the families as a unit in the afterlife as:[150]

رَبَّنَا وَأَدْخِلْهُمْ جَنَّاتِ عَدْنٍ الَّتِي وَعَدتَّهُم وَمَن صَلَحَ مِنْ آبَائِهِمْ وَأَزْوَاجِهِمْ وَذُرِّيَّاتِهِمْ إِنَّكَ أَنتَ الْعَزِيزُ الْحَكِيمُ {غافر/8}

Therefore, in today's societies endowments, one can find mostly religious family endowment funds with the intention of pleasing Allah ﷻ. The best examples of these funds are ahlu-bayt, a'l-Muhammad ﷺ, the family of Rasulullah ﷺ, āl-Ibrahim (عليه السلام), the family Ibrahim (عليه السلام), all other prophets, Yaqub (عليه السلام), Isa (عليه السلام), Musa (عليه السلام), Zakariya (عليه السلام), Yahya (عليه السلام), Maryam (عليه السلام), Ismail (عليه السلام), Ishaq (عليه السلام), Harun (عليه السلام) and all other prophets,(عليهم السلام).

The specific mention of Āl-Imran as a Sûrah name can indicate and emphasize the importance of collective need for families working together to achieve the same goal as a family endowment or as a sadaqa-I Jariya as a silsila, from one generation to another generation.

---

148. So [Solomon] smiled, amused at her speech, and said, "My Lord, enable me to be grateful for Your favor which You have bestowed upon me and upon my parents and to do righteousness of which You approve. And admit me by Your mercy into [the ranks of] Your righteous servants."

149. And We have enjoined upon man, to his parents, good treatment. His mother carried him with hardship and gave birth to him with hardship, and his gestation and weaning [period] is thirty months. [He grows] until, when he reaches maturity and reaches [the age of] forty years, he says, "My Lord, enable me to be grateful for Your favor which You have bestowed upon me and upon my parents and to work righteousness of which You will approve and make righteous for me my offspring. Indeed, I have repented to You, and indeed, I am of the Muslims."

150. Our Lord, and admit them to gardens of perpetual residence which You have promised them and whoever was righteous among their fathers, their spouses and their offspring. Indeed, it is You who is the Exalted in Might, the Wise.

Juz 20

Sûrah 28 – al-Qasas

[5]

وَنُرِيدُ أَن نَّمُنَّ عَلَى الَّذِينَ اسْتُضْعِفُوا فِي الْأَرْضِ وَنَجْعَلَهُمْ أَئِمَّةً وَنَجْعَلَهُمُ الْوَارِثِينَ {57/القصص}[151]

La ilaha illa Allah: the Essence

When we analyze the lives of the people who are oppressed in the realities of the purpose of the life, one can feel hopeless, and pessimistic.

Yet, when we think about the life similar to a journey on the sea or ocean, we are traveling regardless of the condition of the sea. Then, the person can focus to the purpose, meaning and goal regardless of the conditions of a sunny day, a cold day, a dark day, a rainy day, a snow day and the external conditions of the day.

The externalities affect our motions. Sometimes, it helps us to focus to a purpose, meaning and goal. Sometimes and maybe most of the time, the conditions or these externalities actually distract us. We happen to change our purpose, goal or meaning constantly with the changing external conditions.

In this regard, the achievements on the earth, having power and even establishing justice, peace, moral and ethical life can be all externalities but not the real internality, goal and the purpose.

One can review the ayah وَنُرِيدُ أَن نَّمُنَّ عَلَى الَّذِينَ اسْتُضْعِفُوا فِي الْأَرْضِ وَنَجْعَلَهُمْ أَئِمَّةً وَنَجْعَلَهُمُ الْوَارِثِينَ {5/القصص} with the ayah below as:

وَعَدَ اللَّهُ الَّذِينَ آمَنُوا مِنكُمْ وَعَمِلُوا الصَّالِحَاتِ لَيَسْتَخْلِفَنَّهُم فِي الْأَرْضِ كَمَا اسْتَخْلَفَ الَّذِينَ مِن قَبْلِهِمْ وَلَيُمَكِّنَنَّ لَهُمْ دِينَهُمُ الَّذِي ارْتَضَى لَهُمْ وَلَيُبَدِّلَنَّهُم مِّن بَعْدِ خَوْفِهِمْ أَمْنًا يَعْبُدُونَنِي لَا يُشْرِكُونَ بِي شَيْئًا وَمَن كَفَرَ بَعْدَ ذَلِكَ فَأُولَئِكَ هُمُ الْفَاسِقُونَ {55/النور}[152]

---

151. And We wanted to confer favor upon those who were oppressed in the land and make them leaders and make them inheritors

152. Allah has promised those who have believed among you and done righteous deeds that He will surely grant them succession [to authority] upon the earth just as He granted it to those before them and that He will surely establish for them [therein] their religion which He has preferred for them and that He will surely substitute for them, after their fear, security, [for] they worship Me, not associating anything with Me. But whoever disbelieves after that—then those are the defiantly disobedient.

Allah ﷻ gives the people of imān what they desire as mentioned وَعَدَ اللَّهُ الَّذِينَ آمَنُوا مِنكُمْ وَعَمِلُوا الصَّالِحَاتِ لَيَسْتَخْلِفَنَّهُم فِي الْأَرْضِ كَمَا اسْتَخْلَفَ الَّذِينَ مِن قَبْلِهِمْ

Yet, in the personal encounters of life as one is sailing in this sea of life, the boat does not stop but continues.

In this journey, the essence is La ilaha illa Allah. The essence is regardless of the externalities one's boat is still moving. In this journey, the essence La ilaha illa Allah requires focusing on Allah ﷻ and leaving everything as they are all distractions.

In good conditions, such as in the conditions of a Muslims having a peaceful place, state and conditions of living a life according to وَلَيُمَكِّنَنَّ لَهُمْ دِينَهُمُ الَّذِي ارْتَضَى لَهُمْ وَلَيُبَدِّلَنَّهُم مِّن بَعْدِ خَوْفِهِمْ أَمْنًا, the personal journey or the personal boat of life is still moving.

In all conditions, one should focus on the essence, La ilaha illa Allah. This requires يَعْبُدُونَنِي لَا يُشْرِكُونَ بِي شَيْئًا. The Dhat mentioned with the pronoun نَنِي in يَعْبُدُونَنِي and بِي in لَا يُشْرِكُونَ بِي شَيْئًا can indicate this essence of La ilaha illa Allah in the good-looking conditions of externalities especially in the context of this ayah as وَلَيُمَكِّنَنَّ لَهُمْ دِينَهُمُ الَّذِي ارْتَضَى لَهُمْ وَلَيُبَدِّلَنَّهُم مِّن بَعْدِ خَوْفِهِمْ أَمْنًا.

Even in these conditions of good-looking externalities where a person can live the life and practice their religion with bounties and ease, still the personal boat or journey continues. Even, in these conditions, there are the ones who are still distracted and defocused as mentioned[153] وَمَن كَفَرَ بَعْدَ ذَلِكَ فَأُوْلَئِكَ هُمُ الْفَاسِقُونَ {النور /55}.

This reality can teach us that the essence La ilaha illa Allah is not dependent on the conditions. La ilaha illa Allah is essential and independent unchanging reality. Therefore, no one can claim or put any condition in front of La ilaha illa Allah to embody, realize and adapt this essence.

In this sense, no one can place the difficulty of the externalities and claiming weakness in order not to embody this essence as mentioned[154]

---

153. Allah has promised those who have believed among you and done righteous deeds that He will surely grant them succession [to authority] upon the earth just as He granted it to those before them and that He will surely establish for them [therein] their religion which He has preferred for them and that He will surely substitute for them, after their fear, security, [for] they worship Me, not associating anything with Me. But whoever disbelieves after that—then those are the defiantly disobedient.

154. Indeed, those whom the angels take [in death] while wronging themselves—[the angels] will say, "In what [condition] were you?" They will say, "We were oppressed in the land." The angels will say, "Was not the earth of Allah spacious [enough] for you to emigrate therein?" For those, their refuge is Hell—and evil it is as a destination.

إِنَّ الَّذِينَ تَوَفَّاهُمُ الْمَلَائِكَةُ ظَالِمِي أَنْفُسِهِمْ قَالُوا فِيمَ كُنتُمْ قَالُوا كُنَّا مُسْتَضْعَفِينَ فِي الأَرْضِ قَالُوا أَلَمْ تَكُنْ أَرْضُ اللّهِ وَاسِعَةً فَتُهَاجِرُوا فِيهَا فَأُوْلَـئِكَ مَأْوَاهُمْ جَهَنَّمُ وَسَاءتْ مَصِيرًا {النساء/97}

If the externalities become difficult for the embodiment of this essence, then the person moves on from this externality as mentioned in the previous ayah make mujahadah and hijrah.

Rasulullah ﷺ teaches us to ask Allah ﷻ to have an easy life but not ask difficulties and tests. In all externally good or bad, easy or difficult looking conditions, conditions are externalities and secondary. The essence is La ilaha illa Allah.

Some of the mutasawwifun from the salaf expressed La ilaha illa Allah as the pleasure of Allah ﷻ, as the Rida of Allah ﷻ. Some expressed it being in the state of ihsan. Some expressed it being in the constant maqam/statition of fana, annihilation, leaving everything and focusing on Allah ﷻ.

One can look then, the notions of the theodicy, blaming evil and conditions on God, especially in Western approaches of religion.

If we see the externalities as secondary, the conditions become less important than the essence. Yet, at the same time, we follow our Habib ﷺ as we are human, weak and affected by externalities in the encounters of life conditions such as death, imprisonment, torture, sickness, and in all forms external pain.

Rasulullah ﷺ expresses this reality when he ﷺ lost son. When his ﷺ son died, there were tears normalizing our humanness by being affected from the loss of a loved one. Yet, he ﷺ mentioned that his blessed heart ﷺ is in full rida and contentment of the decree of Allah ﷻ. With many other examples in his life ﷺ, this can show the embodiment of La ilaha illa Allah, rida, ihsan and fana in Rasulullah ﷺ.

Yusuf as mentioned this essence of La ilaha illa Allah in an externally evil looking condition of imprisonment as[155] يَا صَاحِبَيِ السِّجْنِ أَأَرْبَابٌ مُّتَفَرِّقُونَ خَيْرٌ أَمِ اللّهُ الْوَاحِدُ الْقَهَّارُ {يوسف/39} مَا تَعْبُدُونَ مِن دُونِهِ إِلاَّ أَسْمَاء سَمَّيْتُمُوهَا أَنتُمْ وَآبَآؤُكُم مَّا أَنزَلَ اللّهُ بِهَا مِن سُلْطَانٍ إِنِ الْحُكْمُ إِلاَّ لِلّهِ أَمَرَ أَلاَّ تَعْبُدُواْ إِلاَّ إِيَّاهُ ذَلِكَ الدِّينُ الْقَيِّمُ وَلَكِنَّ أَكْثَرَ النَّاسِ لاَ يَعْلَمُونَ {يوسف/40}

---

155. O [my] two companions of prison, are separate lords better or Allah, the One, the Prevailing? You worship not besides Him except [mere] names you have named them, you and your fathers, for which Allah has sent down no authority. Legislation is not but for Allah. He has commanded that you worship not except Him. That is the correct religion, but most of the people do not know.

In this regard, one can realize the Name and Attribute of Allah ﷻ as al-Wahid and al-Qahhar as mentioned {يوسف/39} الْوَاحِدُ الْقَهَّارُ can indicate this essential and required focus on La ilaha illa Allah removing oneself from all evil or good-looking multiplicities or deities leading to the One, al-Wahid.

In this sense in Islām in all true forms of Christianity and Judaism, life is not pain or suffering as philosophized in Buddhism. Then, this perspective can bring kufr, pessimism, and darkness in the optimistic perspectives of life for future.

Life in the Qurān, Tawrah, and Injil are all amazements, pleasures and astonishments that constantly emphasize and increase the certainty of the real focus, La ilaha illa Allah.

All the externalities are conditions. Conditions are temporary and changing. They can have a temporary effect on us. Yet, these temporal effects should not affect the essence and the core of La ilaha illa Allah. Essence of La ilaha illa Allah is Independent. All conditions are variables and dependent.

Today, the main problem of theodicy spreading like a disease is mainly due to temporal effects replacing the core with chaos. Temporal effects removing the essence and core and leaving individuals with empty, hollow, and depressed and distracted states of pessimism, and spiritual darkness. Evil and blaming God are all due the mixing of conditions with the real and essential states.

These all perspectives of La ilaha illa Allah can help the person remove oneself from the effects of the diseases of theodicy, especially when one witnesses people going through external difficulties and even when he or she experiences.

The realization, and acceptance of this essence of La ilaha illa Allah referred as iman is given by Allah ﷻ as a Fadl and Grace by Allah.

In this regard, when some of the sahabah were tortured and came to Rasulullah ﷺ complaining about their conditions of torture, Rasulullah ﷺ did not lose himself like us, getting angry with the people, and disturbed or being pessimistic but he reminded the essence that La ilaha illa Allah. The previous nations of Muslims concentrated on this essence of La ilaha illa Allah such as ashab-I ukhdûd, yet their externalities, or conditions of secondary means were worse as reminded to sahabah by Rasulullah [3].

Allah ﷻ showed us mercy by sending the Rahmatan lil alamin Rasulullah ﷺ. He ﷻ taught us to make the dua constantly with "Allahumma inni asaluka afwa wal 'afiya" that we should constantly ask. All the ways of falah goes from and on the path of Rahmatan lil Alamin, Rasulullah ﷺ.

Allah ﷻ showed us Mercy by teaching us the dua in the Qurān as :[156]

رَبَّنَا لاَ تُؤَاخِذْنَا إِن نَّسِينَا أَوْ أَخْطَأْنَا رَبَّنَا وَلاَ تَحْمِلْ عَلَيْنَا إِصْرًا كَمَا حَمَلْتَهُ عَلَى الَّذِينَ مِن قَبْلِنَا رَبَّنَا وَلاَ تُحَمِّلْنَا مَا لاَ طَاقَةَ لَنَا بِهِ وَاعْفُ عَنَّا وَاغْفِرْ لَنَا وَارْحَمْنَآ أَنتَ مَوْلاَنَا فَانصُرْنَا عَلَى الْقَوْمِ الْكَافِرِينَ {البقرة/286}

Rasulullah ﷺ instructed us to read the above ayahs daily after isha [3] [14].

One can also view taklif that it is the endurance capacity of a person against these externalities but still keeping the essence of La ilaha illa Allah. In this regard, as a mercy and fadl from Allah ﷻ, the reality of لاَ يُكَلِّفُ اللّهُ نَفْسًا إِلاَّ وُسْعَهَا لَهَا مَا كَسَبَتْ وَعَلَيْهَا مَا اكْتَسَبَتْ can show that the externalities of this life confronting the essence of La ilaha illa Allah is within the individualized endurance capacity of each person.

May Allah ﷻ make us follow the path of Rasulullah ﷺ.

Allahumma inna asaluka afwa afiyata fi dunya wal akhirah

اللهم انّا أسألُك العَفوَ و العَفِيَة في الدُنيَا وَالاخِرة

Rabbana atina fid dunya hasanatan wa fil akhirati hasanatan wa qina azabbanar….

ربنا آتِنَا في الدُنيَا حَسَنَة و في الآخرة حَسَنَتاً وَقِنَا عَذابَ النَّار[157]

Allahuma La Sahla Illa ma Jaaltu Sahla wa anta tajala al-hazana iza shi'ta sahlan

اللَّهُمَّ لَا سَهْلَ إِلاَّ مَا جَعَلْتَهُ سَهْلًا، وَأَنْتَ تَجْعَلُ الْحَزْنَ إِذَا شِئْتَ سَهْلًا[158]

---

156. Allah does not charge a soul except [with that within] its capacity. It will have [the consequence of] what [good] it has gained, and it will bear [the consequence of] what [evil] it has earned. "Our Lord, do not impose blame upon us if we have forgotten or erred. Our Lord, and lay not upon us a burden like that which You laid upon those before us. Our Lord, and burden us not with that which we have no ability to bear. And pardon us; and forgive us; and have mercy upon us. You are our protector, so give us victory over the disbelieving people."
157. "Our Lord, give us in this world [that which is] good and in the Hereafter [that which is] good and protect us from the punishment of the Fire."
158. O Allah, there is no ease other than what You make easy. If You please You ease sorrow.

Juz 21

Sûrah 33 -al-Ahzâb

[23-24]

مِنَ الْمُؤْمِنِينَ رِجَالٌ صَدَقُوا مَا عَاهَدُوا اللَّهَ عَلَيْهِ فَمِنْهُم مَّن قَضَى نَحْبَهُ وَمِنْهُم مَّن يَنتَظِرُ
وَمَا بَدَّلُوا تَبْدِيلًا {الأحزاب/23}[159] لِيَجْزِيَ اللَّهُ الصَّادِقِينَ بِصِدْقِهِمْ وَيُعَذِّبَ الْمُنَافِقِينَ إِن
شَاءَ أَوْ يَتُوبَ عَلَيْهِمْ إِنَّ اللَّهَ كَانَ غَفُورًا رَّحِيمًا {الأحزاب/24}

High Goals in Life: Spiritual & Physical Activism

One of the critical parts of imān is having a high goal in life. This high goal is between the person and Allah ﷻ. This high goal can be personalized between the person and Allah ﷻ. The expression in the above ayah as عَاهَدُوا اللَّهَ عَلَيْهِ can indicate this possibility of the high goals between the person and Allah ﷻ.

In this regard, this high goal should have some conditions:

1. Intention to please Allah ﷻ
2. Only having this intention for Allah ﷻ.
3. This goal should be according to the Qurān and Sunnah of Rasulullah ﷺ in order to please Allah ﷻ.
4. The person should strive to reach this goal during his or her entire lifelong journey.
5. After the common personalized intention of pleasing Allah ﷻ with this goal, the person choose a path or an action to please Allah ﷻ. This path or action can be different. Yet, they should be all in line with the Qurān and Sunnah of Rasulullah ﷺ.

For example, a person can aim to make a goal of opening schools in the world to make Dawah in order to please Allah ﷻ. Another person can make a goal of establishing charities to help the poor people in the world in order to please Allah ﷻ. The paths and actions can be different

---

159. Among the believers are men true to what they promised Allah. Among them is he who has fulfilled his vow [to the death], and among them is he who awaits [his chance]. And they did not alter [the terms of their commitment] by any alteration— That Allah may reward the truthful for their truth and punish the hypocrites if He wills or accept their repentance. Indeed, Allah is ever Forgiving and Merciful.

but the intention should be all the same as to please only Allah ﷻ. This is called ikhlas, sincerity.

If a person does not have this motivating utopia of a path to please Allah ﷻ, then there can be a passivism even though the person can be a worshipper with imān. Imān requires activism. Spiritual activism in personal 'ibadah indicates engagement in physical activism, being concerned and worrying about others and helping them.

Rasulullah ﷺ was busy mostly in the day time the physical activism helping others, teaching, building relationships, and implementing justice. He ﷺ was busy at night time with 'ibadah in spiritual activism. Yet, Rasulullah ﷺ was an exception. His both day and night were in the embodiment of ihsān, indicating both spiritual and physical activism with Ikhlas only to please Allah ﷻ. Yet, he ﷺ is our role model that we emulate to follow.

Allahumma Ja'alna Nattibu' Sunnata Imamana Muhammad ﷺ, Rasulullah ﷺ, Amìn.

اللهم جَعَلنَا نَتَّبِعُ سُنَّةَ إِمَامَنَا مُحَمَّد ﷺ، رَسُولُ الله ﷺ، آمِين.

Juz 23

Sûrah 37-Al-Sāffāt

[78,108,119,129]

وَتَرَكْنَا عَلَيْهِ فِي الْآخِرِينَ {78/الصافات}[160]

وَتَرَكْنَا عَلَيْهِ فِي الْآخِرِينَ {108/الصافات}[161]

وَتَرَكْنَا عَلَيْهِمَا فِي الْآخِرِينَ {119/الصافات}[162]

وَتَرَكْنَا عَلَيْهِ فِي الْآخِرِينَ {129/الصافات}[163]

When analyze the above ayahs with the ayah of[164] وَاجْعَل لِّي لِسَانَ صِدْقٍ فِي الْآخِرِينَ {48/الشعراء} , one can realize one's own death and their action

---

160. And left for him [favorable mention] among later generations:
161. And We left for him [favorable mention] among later generations:
162. And We left for them [favorable mention] among later generations:
163. And We left for him [favorable mention] among later generation
164. And grant me a reputation of honor among later generations.

of good works, amalu salih in this life and the desire and zeal for these good works to continue after one dies. As one of the sadaqa jariya is good works of a person after one dies it can allude to this reality as mentioned by Rasulullah ﷺ [14].

Yet, one should remember the fine line between making one's intention to please Allah ﷻ and doing the good works only being remembered only in a reputable way. One can ask Allah ﷻ to have the continuous good work of amal even after death with the intention of pleasing Allah ﷻ. Yet, remembrance by humans and deadly spiritual disease of fame is no use among temporal humans if these actions are not within the pleasure of Allah ﷻ. Shaytān has the all the fame from the beginning of the creation of humans until the end of days. Yet, he is a cursed being as will be in Jahannam. May Allah ﷻ protect us from his deceptions, Amìn.

[164-166]

Collective Efforts: Angels and Humans

وَمَا مِنَّا إِلَّا لَهُ مَقَامٌ مَّعْلُومٌ {الصافات/164} وَإِنَّا لَنَحْنُ الصَّافُّونَ {الصافات/165} وَإِنَّا لَنَحْنُ الْمُسَبِّحُونَ {الصافات/166} 165

When we analyze the ayah of {الصافات/561} وَإِنَّا لَنَحْنُ الصَّافُّونَ with the ayah[166] إِنَّ اللَّهَ يُحِبُّ الَّذِينَ يُقَاتِلُونَ فِي سَبِيلِهِ صَفًّا كَأَنَّهُم بُنْيَانٌ مَّرْصُوصٌ {الصف/4}, then one of the commonalities is that both Surahs has the word of saf or sāf indicating jam'ah or acting together in a group in virtuous acts. These two words indicating this critical concept that they were assigned as the name of these two Suwar.

One of the requirements of the group and jam'ah is that the individuals in this group or jam'ah, they remember Allah ﷻ and make Dhikrullah together besides their individual efforts of dhikr as mentioned[167] وَإِنَّا لَنَحْنُ الصَّافُّونَ {الصافات/165} وَإِنَّا لَنَحْنُ الْمُسَبِّحُونَ {الصافات/166}.

In this attitude of togetherness as a collective unit of remembering Allah ﷻ, the model of angels are given as an example for humans as a

---

165. [The angels say], "There is not among us any except that he has a known position. And indeed, we are those who line up [for prayer]. And indeed, we are those who exalt Allah."
166. Indeed, Allah loves those who fight in His cause in a row as though they are a [single] structure joined firmly.
167. And indeed, we are those who line up [for prayer]. And indeed, we are those who exalt Allah."

role model to emulate as mentioned with {الصافات/165} وَإِنَّا لَنَحْنُ الصَّافُّونَ
وَإِنَّا لَنَحْنُ الْمُسَبِّحُونَ {الصافات/166}.

In all of these groups or jam'ah to establish structure and order, there can be different levels as mentioned[168] {الصافات/164} وَمَا مِنَّا إِلاَّ لَهُ مَقَامٌ مَّعْلُومٌ. In the realm of angels, these maqams or levels are assigned by Allah ﷻ that for example Jibril (عليه السلام) has the higher position of proximity with Allah ﷻ and therefore, his position as among all angels is also higher. Other angels can receive directives and orders from Jibril (عليه السلام). In this regard, the angels true ranking can also indicate their true ranks for Allah ﷻ.

In the realm of humans, the external assigned maqams such as Shaykh, Mufti, teacher, leader and others do not necessarily represent this person's real maqam with Allah ﷻ. This shaykh can have a lower position for Allah ﷻ than a regular and ordinary Muslim.

Yet, in virtuous acts of group associations, the person is still expected to follow this leader or teacher to maintain structure and order in order to receive the barakah of Allah ﷻ.

The ayah[169] إِنَّ اللَّهَ يُحِبُّ الَّذِينَ يُقَاتِلُونَ فِي سَبِيلِهِ صَفًّا كَأَنَّهُم بُنيَانٌ مَّرْصُوصٌ {الصف/4} can indicate this reality of acting and struggle of humans own effort of trying to be in Jam'ah or group associations of virtuous acts even though sometimes it may be difficult.

In this regard, one can compare two expressions for both humans and angels. For humans, the expression كَأَنَّهُم بُنيَانٌ مَّرْصُوصٌ is used. The word of mutasābih as كَأَنَّهُم can indicate humans' effort of embodying the struggle of being together as a unit and working collectively to attain a virtuous goal. Our nafs and ego doesn't like others, their efforts and act as a foolish single arrogant entity like Firaw'n or Shaytān.

Yet, the effort of this person in spite of the frictions of his or her nafs, is loved and appreciated by Allah ﷻ as explicitly mentioned with an emphasis إِنَّ اللَّهَ يُحِبُّ.

On the other hand, when we analyze the case of angels acting as a unit, it is a reality but not struggle on their part as mentioned[170] وَإِنَّا لَنَحْنُ

---

168. [The angels say], "There is not among us any except that he has a known position. Indeed, Allah loves those who fight in His cause in a row as though they are a [single] structure joined firmly.

169. Indeed, Allah loves those who fight in His cause in a row as though they are a [single] structure joined firmly.

170. And indeed, we are those who line up [for prayer].

الصَّافُّونَ {الصافات/165}. The structure of Jumla -Ismiyyah with emphasis can indicate this istimrãr of fitrah for angels. Angels are created by Allah ﷻ. As part of the sunnatullah, they naturally adapt being in Jama'ah or group for doing the virtuous acts. In this regard, the highest form of virtuous act for everyone all creation is Dhikrullah as mentioned[171] وَإِنَّا لَنَحْنُ الْمُسَبِّحُونَ {الصافات/166}.

Therefore, one of the struggles that humans should embody among all the collective affairs of good or virtuous is doing the Dhikrullah collectively.

In this regard, the ayah إِنَّ اللَّهَ يُحِبُّ الَّذِينَ يُقَاتِلُونَ فِي سَبِيلِهِ صَفًّا كَأَنَّهُم بُنيَانٌ مَّرْصُوصٌ {الصف/4} can indicate their collective effort and struggle of activism as loved by Allah ﷻ.

The mention of the ayah as[172] وَإِنَّا لَنَحْنُ الْمُسَبِّحُونَ {الصافات/166} can indicate humans needed struggle and effort of collective Dhikrullah to emulate the angels as pleased by Allah ﷻ.

Collective Efforts: Animals

If one analyzes the ayah[173] أَوَلَمْ يَرَوْا إِلَى الطَّيْرِ فَوْقَهُمْ صَافَّاتٍ وَيَقْبِضْنَ مَا يُمْسِكُهُنَّ إِلَّا الرَّحْمَنُ إِنَّهُ بِكُلِّ شَيْءٍ بَصِيرٌ {الملك/19}, Allah ﷻ mentions the collective efforts of being in Jam'ah with the same word as صَافَّاتٍ.

If one really observes the birds, there is a collective effort of migration, flying and working together under a leader. They have a system and structure. The order formed by different shapes in the sky give this critical understanding for humans who constantly observe them and say "look at the birds, how nice they are flying and following a group!" Yet, when it comes to themselves being part of a group, they immediately reserve themselves in doing a good action.

Similarly, today's fields of zoology tell a lot about the structured lives of animals bees with a king, leader being followed in a very nice and efficient organizational structure, ants working efficiently in their social and group system of Jam'ah. We study those but we don't take any heed from them unfortunately.

---

171. And indeed, we are those who exalt Allah."
172. And indeed, we are those who exalt Allah."
173. Do they not see the birds above them with wings outstretched and [sometimes] folded in? None holds them [aloft] except the Most Merciful. Indeed He is, of all things, Seeing.

Collective Dhikrullah

In this regard, the highest form of collective Dhikrullah is Juma/Friday prayer as ordered by Allah ﷻ. This is mentioned[174] يَا أَيُّهَا الَّذِينَ آمَنُوا إِذَا نُودِيَ لِلصَّلَاةِ مِن يَوْمِ الْجُمُعَةِ فَاسْعَوْا إِلَى ذِكْرِ اللَّهِ وَذَرُوا الْبَيْعَ ذَلِكُمْ خَيْرٌ لَّكُمْ إِن كُنتُمْ تَعْلَمُونَ {الجمعة/9}.

Other forms of collective Dhikrullah in the masājid or in other avenues can be part of the collective Dhikrullah and they have a value to be on the path of angels. In this regard, the collective duas, prayers, tarawih prayers, attending lectures and the circles of dhikr are some practical examples of today and the past.

Yet, one should be careful about the present popular trends alienating the individuals from religious institutions and communities and being a self-sufficient spiritual being.

One should realize that Allah ﷻ created us and knows our spiritual and physical needs. As we should maintain our real identity of self with ikhlas and sincerity only and solely for Allah ﷻ, the realities embedded in our creation requires that we maintain communal spiritual practices.

In this regard, Juma prayer, and sunnahs of praying in Jama' in the masjid have the means and purpose to fulfill this craving need of humans. This need is both for men and women. When there were people who prevented women coming to masjid, Rasulullah ﷺ warned them not to prevent women coming to masjid [3].

Even in later generations, when there was a sahabah interacting with a tabìn, the tabìn wanted to prevent some of the women coming to masjid by using some religious reasoning. Yet, the sahabah got angry said to him in a similar expression of "I am telling you that Rasulullah ﷺ warned us not to prevent women coming to masjid and yet, you are trying to do the otherwise, what a bad religious affair!" [3]. Here, the sahabah (ra) got angry because the highest authority of religious law is established with the Qurān and sunnah of Rasulullah ﷺ, yet there were later religious people who unintendedly missed this basic usûl when establishing and popularizing certain teachings.

There can be always exceptions and cases of general rules as also taught to us by Rasulullah ﷺ. Yet, the exceptions should not become

---

174. O you who have believed, when [the adhan] is called for the prayer on the day of Jumu'ah [Friday], then proceed to the remembrance of Allah and leave trade. That is better for you, if you only knew.

a dominant opinion especially at the times, one tries to implement the flexible legal laws of the religion according to the need of the people, culture and the time.

Oceans of Fitnah due to the Absence of Collective Dhikrullah

One should realize that one of the bonding practices that unite the people toward virtuous actions is the practice of collective Dhikrullah. People coming and praying together in the same saf (congregation) regularly bond together to help others.

The people who come together to make dua, read and listen a book related with imãn, the Qurãn and Rasulullah ﷺ can be bonded with the Barakah of Allah ﷻ as mentioned[175] {الصافات/165} وَإِنَّا لَنَحْنُ الصَّافُّونَ وَإِنَّا لَنَحْنُ الْمُسَبِّحُونَ {الصافات/166}.

The absence of collective Dhikrullah is the source of fithnah, dispute, argumentation among people and among Muslims.

Historically, when this bonding disappears in collective efforts of Dhikrullah through Jama'h of Juma' prayers, praying in the masjid, and other types of gatherings, then hearts started flipping in different directions but not collectively. Although these individuals can be very pious in their sole efforts of practice of the religious rituals, the spirit of collective action is lost. Then the barakah of Allah ﷻ on these individuals through acting in a group and jam'ah is lost.

---

175. And indeed, we are those who line up [for prayer]. And indeed, we are those who exalt Allah."

Barakah and Love of Allah ﷻ with Collective Dhikrullah & Activism

Allah ﷻ loves the unit, group and jam'ah who act collectively in Dhikrullah and collective activism as mentioned[176] إِنَّ اللَّهَ يُحِبُّ الَّذِينَ يُقَاتِلُونَ فِي سَبِيلِهِ صَفًّا كَأَنَّهُم بُنيَانٌ مَّرْصُوصٌ {الصف/4}. When Allah ﷻ loves a group or unit, Allah ﷻ gives barakah on them.

When Allah ﷻ loves them acting in group and collective efforts of good in collective activism and collective Dhikrullah, then Allah ﷻ calls Jibril (عليه السلام) to love them as mentioned in the hadith [3]. Then, Jibril (عليه السلام) loves them. Then, as the leader and highest status of the angels, Jibril (عليه السلام) mentioned as[177] وَمَا مِنَّا إِلَّا لَهُ مَقَامٌ مَّعْلُومٌ {الصافات/164} announces all other angels and all being on the earth to love this group and unit, Jam'ah. Then, there is the love, barakah, easiness, and openings given to this jam'ah, group, and unit by Allah ﷻ with the Grace, Fadl and Rahmah of Allah ﷻ.

The extend of this barakah and openings is in such an extent that even a person who has a wrong intention of being in that group, unit or Jam'ah is forgiven by Allah ﷻ and considered to be included with this group due to this All-Encompassing Barakah and Love of Allah ﷻ for this unit, Jam'ah and group.

May Allah ﷻ make us be part of a group, Jam'ah and unit doing virtuous acts trying to please Allah ﷻ.

May Allah ﷻ make us be part of a group, Jam'ah and unit that Allah ﷻ is pleased with it.

May Allah ﷻ make us to support any collective effort or any group trying to do something good to please Allah ﷻ,

May Allah ﷻ protect us from the hasad of others and hasad of ourselves harming others.

May Allah ﷻ protect us from the harm of visible and invisible beings, their open and secret plots, Amin…Walhamdulillahi Rabbil Alamin, Allahumma Salli ala sayyidina wa Imamana wa Habibina, al-Mustafa ﷺ آمِين… وَالْحَمْدُلله رَبِّ الْعَلَمِين، اللهم صَلِّ عَلَى سَيِّدِنَا وَ اِمَامَنَا وَحَبِيبَنَا، الْمُصطَفى ﷺ

---

176. Indeed, Allah loves those who fight in His cause in a row as though they are a [single] structure joined firmly.

177. [The angels say], "There is not among us any except that he has a known position.

Juz 26

Sûrah 51- Al-Zariyât

[24-26]

هَلْ أَتَاكَ حَدِيثُ ضَيْفِ إِبْرَاهِيمَ الْمُكْرَمِينَ {الذاريات/24} إِذْ دَخَلُوا عَلَيْهِ فَقَالُوا سَلَامًا قَالَ
سَلَامٌ قَوْمٌ مُنكَرُونَ {الذاريات/25}[178] فَرَاغَ إِلَى أَهْلِهِ فَجَاء بِعِجْلٍ سَمِينٍ {الذاريات/26}

Futuwwah

When look at the above ayahs, one can realize that futuwwah does not depend on the age. It is mentioned in tafasir that Ibrahim (عليه السلام) was in his very old age. Yet, when he had a guest with his old age, he tried to entertain them with the etiquettes of futuwwah, cooking, bringing them food and encouraging them to eat. The futuwwah of honoring guest requires focusing on the guest, serving and honoring them, and changing our schedule around the comfort of the guest.

Futuwwah Examples: Honoring the Guests

If we only analyze the notion of futuwwah around the etiquettes of guest, one can realize many ayahs emphasizing this reality:[179]

وَجَاءهُ قَوْمُهُ يُهْرَعُونَ إِلَيْهِ وَمِن قَبْلُ كَانُواْ يَعْمَلُونَ السَّيِّئَاتِ قَالَ يَا قَوْمِ هَؤُلاء بَنَاتِي هُنَّ
أَطْهَرُ لَكُمْ فَاتَّقُواْ اللّهَ وَلاَ تُخْزُونِ فِي ضَيْفِي أَلَيْسَ مِنكُمْ رَجُلٌ رَّشِيدٌ {هود/78}

قَالَ إِنَّ هَؤُلاء ضَيْفِي فَلاَ تَفْضَحُونِ {الحجر/68}[180]

   In the above ayahs, Lût (عليه السلام) reminding the etiquettes of the futuwwah with the guests to stop them from their evil.

   On the other hand, although the qawm of Lût (عليه السلام) was doing an evil, the Qurān possibly indicates that Allah ﷻ specifies also their

---

178. Has there reached you the story of the honored guests of Abraham?—When they entered upon him and said, "[We greet you with] peace." He answered, "[And upon you] peace, [you are] a people unknown. Then he went to his family and came with a fat [roasted] calf
179. And his people came hastening to him, and before [this] they had been doing evil deeds. He said, "O my people, these are my daughters; they are purer for you. So fear Allah and do not disgrace me concerning my guests. Is there not among you a man of reason?"
180. [Lot] said, "Indeed, these are my guests, so do not shame me.

despotic attitude of their habitual evil towards their guests as mentioned[181] وَلَقَدْ رَاوَدُوهُ عَن ضَيْفِهِ فَطَمَسْنَا أَعْيُنَهُمْ فَذُوقُوا عَذَابِي وَنُذُرِ {القمر/37}.

In other words, one can remember prior ayahs that Lut as tried to stop them by reminding them the etiquettes of the futuwwah with guests but they did not stop, then a harsh punishment is mentioned as فَطَمَسْنَا أَعْيُنَهُمْ فَذُوقُوا عَذَابِي وَنُذُرِ.

In this sense, one can consider and realize that there are vulnerable and weak population. Some of them can be orphans, women, old people, children and guests due to traveling and being in need. When we review the Qurān and hadith of Rasulullah ﷺ, there is very harsh punishment against the people who harms these weak and needy groups. This can be because of their vulnerability for being potentially abused due to their weakness and needs. This can be their vulnerability because they are in need therefore they can allow and permit abuse on them. They can be weak financially and physically such as the women, orphans and old people. They can be weak emotionally and mentally, financially and physically such as the children or even animals. Rasulullah ﷺ warned people who abuse animals [3] with harsh punishment, SubhanAllah![182]

فَانطَلَقَا حَتَّى إِذَا أَتَيَا أَهْلَ قَرْيَةٍ اسْتَطْعَمَا أَهْلَهَا فَأَبَوْا أَن يُضَيِّفُوهُمَا فَوَجَدَا فِيهَا جِدَارًا يُرِيدُ أَنْ يَنقَضَّ فَأَقَامَهُ قَالَ لَوْ شِئْتَ لَاتَّخَذْتَ عَلَيْهِ أَجْرًا {الكهف/77}

In the case of Khidr as and Musa as, the ayah mentions absence of the etiquette of the futuwwah of the guests. Yet, Khidr as does something good and virtuous of building the wall regardless of their absence of futuwwah of the guests in that village.

Futuwwah and True Piety

Futuwwah requires taking a physical action. Physical action to fulfill a need is related with piety and taqwa of Allah ﷻ. Passivism at the time of need can be related with laziness even though the person or people are known to be pious.

---

181. And they had demanded from him his guests, but We obliterated their eyes, [saying], "Taste My punishment and warning."

182. So they set out, until when they came to the people of a town, they asked its people for food, but they refused to offer them hospitality. And they found therein a wall about to collapse, so al-Khidr restored it. [Moses] said, "If you wished, you could have taken for it a payment."

Social classes that give people certain expectations of activism depending on the level of the person instill arrogance, laziness, separation of the elite from everyday problem of the common people or public.

Therefore, in true religious affairs, activism is part of the true piety in one's relationship with Allah ﷻ. The type of activism does not depend on the level of the social class of the activist but true and sincere activism is for the sake of Allah ﷻ and it is fulfilling the need of the person or people at any time. When we review the Islamic law, that is also based on these principles.

For example, there can be a pious person or people, if someone is moving their house and they need help, the true piety requires helping this person to move his or her house but not spend time in the masjid or mosque for extra nawafil prayers. The so-called pious person cannot hide behind his piety and assume and internalize that what he or she is doing much more important than helping that person.

At least if the person cannot help, he should encourage others to help and feel guilty that he was not able to help the person who was in need.

Activism without imān and with imān (Futuwwah)

Activism with imān is called futuwwah.

In some type of life perspectives related with activism, sometimes a question may arise as: are the non-religious activists better than religious people?" How do we understand activism without imān?

In other words, there are people who may not give much importance to the religious affairs that connect people to Allah ﷻ with the avenues of imān, the Qurān and sunnah of Rasulullah ﷺ. Yet, they seem to dedicate their lives to activism, and helping others. How do we understand this?

First, one should remember that Rasulullah ﷺ was the most active activist helping the poor and in need regardless of their belief or faith both before and after the prophethood. Some scholars even consider that his ﷺ utmost concern of helping others also can be another hikmah or wisdom besides many others made him ﷺ to be the chosen one in the Divine Qadar of Allah ﷻ.

Yet, although activism is great to relieve the people from their difficulties, the real meaning of activism presents and becomes permanent both in this life and afterlife with intention and purpose.

A person who does not recognize Allah ﷻ may try to help others. Yet, if he or she does not recognize Allah ﷻ purposefully and by deliberate choice, then this itself is an ungrateful and unappreciation attitude leading to evil. Therefore, this person him or herself actually needs help.

Most of the time, the fruits of our activism give us satisfaction of seeing others happy. Yet, most of the time, the person or an activist is in the verge of internal struggles through their own self, ego, nafs with the notions of purpose in life, reality of dead, the realities of uncontrolled and unexpected events in his or her life and lives of others. In reality, this activist person in real his or her real self is in detrimental spiritual chaos. They need an urgent and immediate help.

How can an empty cup give water or true life to others with true hope if there is no imān? Imān is hope. Hope is imān. There is no hope if there is no imān. There is no true imān if there is no hope. Knowing that everything is in control of Allah ﷻ with imān gives hope to the person. How can a person live a life if he or she knows the reality of the earth spinning and rotating around different axis's with thousands of miles of speed? If there is a microscopic deviation on the orbit, everything will explode, and we will be turned into dust. Yet, imān requires that Allah ﷻ shows us that Allah ﷻ controls and maintains everything among all those impossibilities. This is imān. This gives hope. Absence of imān gives pessimism, darkness and chaos.

Therefore, the ideal activism is with imān, action, amalu-salih, and helping everyone and everything in need. Therefore, the Qurān repeats imān with amalu-salih. Imān requires activism, helping others.

In Islām, a niceness is sadaqa. If a person helps another financially but does not show the attitude of niceness, then showing kindness, niceness and hope is preferred over financial help if both won't be maintained together. This is explicitly mentioned in the Qurān as:[183] قَوْلٌ

مَّعْرُوفٌ وَمَغْفِرَةٌ خَيْرٌ مِّن صَدَقَةٍ يَتْبَعُهَآ أَذًى وَاللَّهُ غَنِيٌّ حَلِيمٌ {البقرة/263}

---

183. Kind speech and forgiveness are better than charity followed by injury. And Allah is Free of need and Forbearing.

Similarly, an activist who cannot give hope with the discourses of imān but only help physically cannot be at the ideal level of helping others.

All the conversations, words, or explanations of hope that are disconnecting the person from Allah ﷻ are not hope. They are poisonous honey. They look good in the beginning for the patient but kills them later.

Similarly, conversations, teachings and discourses of hope related with imān and connecting the person to Allah ﷻ is the real medicine. Both its inside and outside is honey and sweet. This type of hope and help elevates the person in this life and afterlife.

There are a lot of people from our pious salaf who were elevated from lower ranks to higher ranks with the real hope of imān.

Omar ra mentions that "we are elevated with Islām-imān" [11][184]. This is a reality. He ra and other sahabah mentioned how Allah ﷻ elevated them with imān-Islām, the true source of hope.

Juz 28

Sûrah 61 Al-Saf

[4]

{إِنَّ اللَّهَ يُحِبُّ الَّذِينَ يُقَاتِلُونَ فِي سَبِيلِهِ صَفًّا كَأَنَّهُم بُنيَانٌ مَّرْصُوصٌ} [185]{الصف/4}

When we analyze the above ayah with the ayah of[186] {وَإِنَّا لَنَحْنُ الصَّافُّونَ} {الصافات/165}, one of the commonalities is that both Surahs has the word of saf or sāf indicating jam'ah or acting together in a group in virtuous acts. These two words indicating this critical concept that they were assigned as the name of these two Sûrah.

---

184. al-Mustadrak 214
185. Indeed, Allah loves those who fight in His cause in a row as though they are a [single] structure joined firmly.
186. And indeed, we are those who line up [for prayer].

Juz 29

Sûrah 74 -Al-Mudassir

{كَلَّا إِنَّهُ كَانَ لِآيَاتِنَا عَنِيدًا {المدثر/16} سَأُرْهِقُهُ صَعُودًا {المدثر/17}[187]

إِنَّهُ فَكَّرَ وَقَدَّرَ {المدثر/18} فَقُتِلَ كَيْفَ قَدَّرَ {المدثر/19} ثُمَّ قُتِلَ كَيْفَ قَدَّرَ {المدثر/20} ثُمَّ نَظَرَ {المدثر/21} ثُمَّ عَبَسَ وَبَسَرَ {المدثر/22} ثُمَّ أَدْبَرَ وَاسْتَكْبَرَ {المدثر/23} فَقَالَ إِنْ هَذَا إِلَّا سِحْرٌ يُؤْثَرُ {المدثر/24} إِنْ هَذَا إِلَّا قَوْلُ الْبَشَرِ {المدثر/25}

If we analyze the above ayahs, then we can realize that there is the reality of a person's thinking, analysis and deductions. The person's deduction is إِنْ هَذَا إِلَّا قَوْلُ الْبَشَرِ {المدثر/25}.

Then, we can compare above ayahs with another set of ayahs of the Qurān with a different result and deduction as[188] إِنَّ فِي خَلْقِ السَّمَاوَاتِ وَالْأَرْضِ وَاخْتِلَافِ اللَّيْلِ وَالنَّهَارِ لَآيَاتٍ لِأُولِي الْأَلْبَابِ {آل عمران/190} الَّذِينَ يَذْكُرُونَ اللَّهَ قِيَامًا وَقُعُودًا وَعَلَىٰ جُنُوبِهِمْ وَيَتَفَكَّرُونَ فِي خَلْقِ السَّمَاوَاتِ وَالْأَرْضِ رَبَّنَا مَا خَلَقْتَ هَذَا بَاطِلًا سُبْحَانَكَ فَقِنَا عَذَابَ النَّارِ {آل عمران/191} رَبَّنَا إِنَّكَ مَن تُدْخِلِ النَّارَ فَقَدْ أَخْزَيْتَهُ وَمَا لِلظَّالِمِينَ مِنْ أَنصَارٍ {آل عمران/192} رَبَّنَا إِنَّنَا سَمِعْنَا مُنَادِيًا يُنَادِي لِلْإِيمَانِ أَنْ آمِنُوا بِرَبِّكُمْ فَآمَنَّا رَبَّنَا فَاغْفِرْ لَنَا ذُنُوبَنَا وَكَفِّرْ عَنَّا سَيِّئَاتِنَا وَتَوَفَّنَا مَعَ الْأَبْرَارِ {آل عمران/193} رَبَّنَا وَآتِنَا مَا وَعَدتَّنَا عَلَىٰ رُسُلِكَ وَلَا تُخْزِنَا يَوْمَ الْقِيَامَةِ إِنَّكَ لَا تُخْلِفُ الْمِيعَادَ {آل عمران/194}

One can ask what is the difference and similarity in above two cases? First, we need to analyze a few very key concepts in human's reality of existence.

---

187. No! Indeed, he has been toward Our verses obstinate. I will cover him with arduous torment. Indeed, he thought and deliberated. So may he be destroyed [for] how he deliberated. Then he considered [again]; Then he frowned and scowled; Then he turned back and was arrogant And said, "This is not but magic imitated [from others]. This is not but the word of a human being."

188. Indeed, in the creation of the heavens and the earth and the alternation of the night and the day are signs for those of understanding. Who remember Allah while standing or sitting or [lying] on their sides and give thought to the creation of the heavens and the earth, [saying], "Our Lord, You did not create this aimlessly; exalted are You [above such a thing]; then protect us from the punishment of the Fire. Our Lord, indeed whoever You admit to the Fire—You have disgraced him, and for the wrongdoers there are no helpers. Our Lord, indeed whoever You admit to the Fire—You have disgraced him, and for the wrongdoers there are no helpers. Our Lord, indeed we have heard a caller calling to faith, [saying], 'Believe in your Lord,' and we have believed. Our Lord, so forgive us our sins and remove from us our misdeeds and cause us to die with the righteous. Our Lord, and grant us what You promised us through Your messengers and do not disgrace us on the Day of Resurrection. Indeed, You do not fail in [Your] promise."

The Reality of Constant Function of the Brain: Thinking, Judging, Analyzing & Deducing

One of our involuntary actions is constant thinking. We cannot stop our brain, thinking, judging, analyzing and deducing meanings and results.

Then, one can ask what is the hikmah-wisdom of this brain function given to us as an involuntary and uncontrolled action in our system as a human by Allah ﷻ?

Islamic legal system is all rulings and based on a being called human with the condition of full and intact brain and mind. If a person is crazy or insane, the legal rulings fail and do not apply.

One of the things that differentiate us from other beings is our aqil, mind, and intellect. Thinking, judging, analyzing and deducing are all qualities of aqil, mind or intellect.

For example, animals and other beings have inspirations (wahiy as the Qurān refers) about their intrinsic knowledge given by Allah ﷻ. In our modern terms, they are programmed in their intrinsic qualities according to their species. A bee is programmed by Allah ﷻ as a type of wahiy to make honey.

Yet, all the animals, and other beings including angels, skies, earth, galaxies, planets are in constant state of Dhikrullah with different types of tasbìh, tahmìd, and takbir and all different forms of dhikr that we may not understand as mentioned in the Qurān as[189] أَلَمْ تَرَ أَنَّ اللَّهَ يُسَبِّحُ لَهُ مَن فِي السَّمَاوَاتِ وَالْأَرْضِ وَالطَّيْرُ صَافَّاتٍ كُلٌّ قَدْ عَلِمَ صَلَاتَهُ وَتَسْبِيحَهُ وَاللَّهُ عَلِيمٌ بِمَا يَفْعَلُونَ {النور/41}.

In the realm of the humans, this constant intrinsic dhikr of all other beings given by Allah ﷻ can transform or project into the constant involuntary engagements of thinking, judging, analyzing and deducing meanings and results through the engagements of the brain.

In other words, the intrinsic or involuntary given state of continuous Dhikrullah bestowed on all beings excepts humans and Jinn project on our plane of reality as cognition or thinking as the faculties of aqìl or mind.

The result of this continuous Dhikrullah of all other beings put them in constant sakina states calmness, peace, happiness, and tranquility.

---

189. Do you not see that Allah is exalted by whomever is within the heavens and the earth and [by] the birds with wings spread [in flight]? Each [of them] has known his [means of] prayer and exalting [Him], and Allah is Knowing of what they do.

The result of humans' continuous state of thinking, judging, analyzing, and deducing meanings and taking an action puts the humans in different states of emotions.

The main reason of humans given involuntary state of thinking, judging, analyzing, and deducing meanings require to acquire knowledge, I'lm. The purpose of requiring all the knowledge, ilm is to acquire the Real I'lm, Marifatullah. The I'lm related with Allah ﷻ.

Yet, Allah ﷻ is al-Bakì. The il'm related with Allah ﷻ is infinite as mentioned[190] قُل لَّوْ كَانَ الْبَحْرُ مِدَادًا لِّكَلِمَاتِ رَبِّي لَنَفِدَ الْبَحْرُ قَبْلَ أَن تَنفَدَ كَلِمَاتُ رَبِّي وَلَوْ جِئْنَا بِمِثْلِهِ مَدَدًا {الكهف/109}

وَلَوْ أَنَّمَا فِي الْأَرْضِ مِن شَجَرَةٍ أَقْلَامٌ وَالْبَحْرُ يَمُدُّهُ مِن بَعْدِهِ سَبْعَةُ أَبْحُرٍ مَّا نَفِدَتْ كَلِمَاتُ اللَّهِ إِنَّ اللَّهَ عَزِيزٌ حَكِيمٌ {لقمان/27}[191]

Yet, with this I'lm humans have the possibility of surpassing and exceeding all the creation including angels as mentioned[192] وَلَقَدْ كَرَّمْنَا بَنِي آدَمَ وَحَمَلْنَاهُمْ فِي الْبَرِّ وَالْبَحْرِ وَرَزَقْنَاهُم مِّنَ الطَّيِّبَاتِ وَفَضَّلْنَاهُمْ عَلَى كَثِيرٍ مِّمَّنْ خَلَقْنَا تَفْضِيلاً {الإسراء/70}.

Yet, acquiring the true I'lm leading to Marifatullah is also with Permission, Fadl, Tawfiq and Grace of Allah ﷻ as mentioned in Sûrah Baqara (255) in ayatal Kursi as وَلاَ يُحِيطُونَ بِشَيْءٍ مِّنْ عِلْمِهِ إِلاَّ بِمَا شَاء.

On the other hand, for a person, there is the possibility of going lower than all beings if they don't use their free-will in the correct acquirement about the Marifatullah as mentioned[193] إِنَّا عَرَضْنَا الْأَمَانَةَ عَلَى السَّمَاوَاتِ وَالْأَرْضِ وَالْجِبَالِ فَأَبَيْنَ أَن يَحْمِلْنَهَا وَأَشْفَقْنَ مِنْهَا وَحَمَلَهَا الْإِنسَانُ إِنَّهُ كَانَ ظَلُومًا جَهُولًا {الأحزاب/72}

---

190. Say, "If the sea were ink for [writing] the words of my Lord, the sea would be exhausted before the words of my Lord were exhausted, even if We brought the like of it as a supplement."
191. And if whatever trees upon the earth were pens and the sea [was ink], replenished thereafter by seven [more] seas, the words of Allah would not be exhausted. Indeed, Allah is Exalted in Might and Wise.
192. And We have certainly honored the children of Adam and carried them on the land and sea and provided for them of the good things and preferred them over much of what We have created, with [definite] preference.
193. Indeed, we offered the Trust to the heavens and the earth and the mountains, and they declined to bear it and feared it; but man [undertook to] bear it. Indeed, he was unjust and ignorant.

١٩٤{التين/5} لَقَدْ خَلَقْنَا الْإِنسَانَ فِي أَحْسَنِ تَقْوِيمٍ {التين/4} ثُمَّ رَدَدْنَاهُ أَسْفَلَ سَافِلِينَ {التين/5}١٩٤

When humans acquire and be on the path of acquirement of marifatullah, they can be at higher states of sakina than other beings as mentioned by one of the salaf (Kutbul Arsh).

When they don't acquire this knowledge, and use this involuntary function of thinking, analysis, and judgment in an improper way such as causing nifâq, fisq, negligence or indulgence in the world, then the person can be in the worst states of fear, anxiety, stress leading to spiritual even sometimes physical committing suicide compared to the peaceful states of sakina with Marifatullah.

Yes, as humans we accepted to take the advanced credit of pleasing Allah ﷻ at a further level as mentioned in the ayah of Qawlu Bala.

Yes, this is not a gambling but it is a privilege given by Allah ﷻ to go further in the self journey on the path of Allah ﷻ as mentioned[195] لَقَدْ

وَلَقَدْ كَرَّمْنَا بَنِي آدَمَ وَحَمَلْنَاهُمْ فِي الْبَرِّ وَالْبَحْرِ and[196]خَلَقْنَا الْإِنسَانَ فِي أَحْسَنِ تَقْوِيمٍ {التين/4}

وَرَزَقْنَاهُم مِّنَ الطَّيِّبَاتِ وَفَضَّلْنَاهُمْ عَلَىٰ كَثِيرٍ مِّمَّنْ خَلَقْنَا تَفْضِيلاً {الأسراء/70}

Sayri-Fillah, Fana, and Sayr MinAllah

The notions of fana, annihilation is both experiential and knowledge-based acquirement of marifatullah when traveler is on the path of al-Bakì, Allah ﷻ.

This annihilation is normal because after a point, the self, ego or nafs preventing the person to go further in the journey of Marifatullah, need to only realize the Only Absolute Infinite Reality, Allah ﷻ. Therefore, the nafs, ego or the self need to disappear, dissolve or annihilated as translated as fana. Our nafs is only a tool to realize the One, Al-Bakì, Allah ﷻ. When the person goes faster on the journey, these tools can be heavy and can slow down the person. Therefore, it should be left with respect and honor.

---

194. We have certainly created man in the best of stature; Then We return him to the lowest of the low,
195. We have certainly created man in the best of stature;
196. And We have certainly honored the children of Adam and carried them on the land and sea and provided for them of the good things and preferred them over much of what We have created, with [definite] preference.

The scholars of tasawwuf mentions taking this tool again not to serve oneself but to serve others in the coming back of fana state referred as sayri min Allah.

The tool of nafs is there in the journey of sayri illa Allah to have the true Marifatullah. In the state of fana fillah, there is no tool of the nafs. It dissappers or left behind. In this state of fana, everything shows Allah ﷻ. Some people can stay there like Hallaj (rh).

Some can come like the epitome of all role models, Rasulullah ﷺ to humans after mirāj referred as sayri min Allah.

In this state, the person like Rasulullah ﷺ uses the nafs to be with people. Yet, he ﷺ sometimes does emphasize his ﷺ uniqueness with exceptional pracrices of sawmu wisāl. This proves the point of servititude of nafs only being present to serve by being people and acting like them. At another occasion, he ﷺ mentions if you knew what I knew you would laugh less and cry a lot." In the maqam of sayri fillah, the person internally embodies ihsān. Yet, his external is with people and looks normal and ordinary.

The high levels gained during this journey especially at the stations of fana can have terms or notions such as fa kana qaba qawsayn as mentioned in the Qurān. This can project this journey with a language for our human social consruction for the epitome of all role models, Rasulullah ﷺ, al-Habìb ﷺ.

Arrogance Vs Taqwa Related Results After Analysis

In this journey of knowledge, the acquirement or the levels do not depend on a person to be genius. A genius person can make wrong and incorrect analysis spending and investing all the constant involuntary functions of thinking, judging, analyzing and deducing results on wrong results.

One of the key qualities on the path of the struggle is humbleness and humility. A genius person with arrogance fails as mentioned:[197]

قَالَ يَا إِبْلِيسُ مَا مَنَعَكَ أَن تَسْجُدَ لِمَا خَلَقْتُ بِيَدَيَّ أَسْتَكْبَرْتَ أَمْ كُنتَ مِنَ الْعَالِينَ {ص/75}

كَلَّا إِنَّهُ كَانَ لِآيَاتِنَا عَنِيدًا {المدثر/16}[198]

---

197. [Allah] said, "O Iblees, what prevented you from prostrating to that which I created with My hands? Were you arrogant [then], or were you [already] among the haughty?"

198. No! Indeed, he has been toward Our verses obstinate.

In other words, regardless of the knowledge, the starting point of journey on the true path of Marifatullah is the attitude. This attitude is humbleness and humility leading to acceptance after realization.

In the Just, Adl Realm of Allah ﷻ, Allah ﷻ does not make the person responsible if he or she does not realize as mentioned[199] مَّنِ اهْتَدَى فَإِنَّمَا يَهْتَدي لِنَفْسِهِ وَمَن ضَلَّ فَإِنَّمَا يَضِلُّ عَلَيْهَا وَلاَ تَزِرُ وَازِرَةٌ وِزْرَ أُخْرَى وَمَا كُنَّا مُعَذِّبِينَ حَتَّى نَبْعَثَ رَسُولاً {الإسراء/15}

Yet, Allah ﷻ sends constant realization points, incidents, and opportunities in one's lifespan as mentioned[200] سَنُرِيهِمْ آيَاتِنَا فِي الْأَفَاقِ وَفِي أَنفُسِهِمْ حَتَّى يَتَبَيَّنَ لَهُمْ أَنَّهُ الْحَقُّ أَوَلَمْ يَكْفِ بِرَبِّكَ أَنَّهُ عَلَى كُلِّ شَيْءٍ شَهِيدٌ {فصلت/53}.

The critical part is after this realization. The true attitude of humbleness and humility leads to acceptance. This character, attitude or quality of acceptance of the truth and the character, attitude or quality of the rejection of the falsehood is called taqwa. This is mentioned with the word[201] لِّلْمُتَّقِينَ {البقرة/2}.

The person can have the realization, and acceptance attitude and quality of taqwa.[202]

الم {البقرة/1} ذَلِكَ الْكِتَابُ لاَ رَيْبَ فِيهِ هُدًى لِّلْمُتَّقِينَ {البقرة/2} الَّذِينَ يُؤْمِنُونَ بِالْغَيْبِ

The quality or stance or attribute or character of taqwa leads to imān. Then, they have the resulting attitude of الَّذِينَ يُؤْمِنُونَ بِالْغَيْبِ

---

199. Whoever is guided is only guided for [the benefit of] his soul. And whoever errs only errs against it. And no bearer of burdens will bear the burden of another. And never would We punish until We sent a messenger.
200. We will show them Our signs in the horizons and within themselves until it becomes clear to them that it is the truth. But is it not sufficient concerning your Lord that He is, over all things, a Witness?
201. This is the Book about which there is no doubt, a guidance for those conscious of Allah -
202. Alif, Lam, Meem.

BIBLIOGRAPHY

[1] L. W. Sophia Vassipoulou, The Archeological Treasures of Saudi Arabia, University of California, Berkeley, Ernst J. Wasmuth, 2011, p. 198.

[2] U. P. Oxford, "Oxford Dictionaries," 2016. [Online]. Available: http://www.oxforddictionaries.com/us/definition/american_ english/. [Accessed 2016].

[3] A. Muslim, Sahih Muslim (translated by Siddiqui, A.), Peace Vision, 1972.

[4] S. Abu-Dawud, Sunan Abu Dawud, Riyadh: Darussalam, 2008.

[5] I. Majah, Sunan Ibn Majah, Darus-Salam, 2007.

[6] S. Vahide, The Collection of Light, ihlas nur publication, 2001.

[7] A. I. Thalabi, Al-Kashaf wal bayan, Beirut: DKI, 2004.

[8] J. Best, Social Problems, New York: W. W. Norton & Company, Inc., 2013.

[9] R. Murphy, Critical Companion to T. S. Eliot A Literary Reference to His Life and Work, Facts On File, Incorporated, 2007, p. 564.

[10] S. K. Sadr a. Policies, The Economic System of the Early Islamic Period Institutions and Policies, Palgrave Macmillan US, Springer, 2016, p. 23.

[11] M. i. A. Hakim, Al-Mustadrak: `ala al-sahihayn, Dar al-Kutub al-`Ilmiyyah, 1990, p. 612/1.

[12] I. M. Gazzali, Ihya Ulum ad-din, Qazi Publicaitons.

[13] R. NADEEM, Buddha As Prophet (a True Biography), Amazon Digital Services LLC—KDP, 2017.

[14] M. Al-Bukhari, The translation of the meanings of Sahih Al-Bukhari, Kazi Publications, 1986.

[15] C. Brazier, Listening to the Other A New Approach to Counselling and Listening Skills, O Books, 2009.

[16] M. I. I. Bukhari, Moral Teachings of Islam: Prophetic Traditions from Al-Adab Al-mufrad, Rowman Altamira, 2003.

[17] M. Tirmizi, Jami At-Tirmizi, Dar-us-Salam, 2007.

[18] K. a. Y. Roberts, Religion in Sociological Perspective. 6th edition, 2017, Sage Publishing, 2017, p. 50.

[19] G. Muhammad, Ijāz of the Quran, Nāyl Publishers, 2008.

AUTHOR BIO

Dr. Kumek had classical training in Islamic sciences from the respected Shuyûqh/Teachers of Turkey, India, Egypt, Yemen, Somalia, Morocco, Sudan, and the United States. He stayed and studied classical Islamic sciences in Egypt and Turkey as well.

In his Western training, education and teaching experience, Dr. Kumek has acted as the religious studies coordinator at State University of New York (SUNY) Buffalo State and taught undergraduate and graduate courses in religious studies at SUNY at Buffalo State, Niagara University, Daemen College and Harvard Divinity School. Dr. Kumek also pursued doctorate degree in physics at SUNY at Buffalo published academic papers in the areas of quantum physics and medical physics. Then, he decided to engage with the world of social sciences through social anthropology, education, and cultural anthropology in his doctorate studies and subsequently, spent a few years as a research associate in the anthropology department of the same university and subsequently, completed a postdoctoral fellowship at Harvard Divinity school. Some of his book titles include sociology through religion, religious literacy through ethnography, selected passages from the Qurãn, selected passages from the Hadith (titled as Rasulullah 鑾) and selected prayers of the Prophet Muhammad 鑾 (titled as Pearls and Diamonds). Dr. M. Yunus Kumek is currently teaching on Muslim Ministry and Spiritual Care at Harvard Divinity School.

ACKNOWLEDGMENTS

I would like to thank all my unnamed teachers, friends, and students for their input, ideas, suggestions, help, and support during and before the preparation of this book.

I would like to thank Dr. David Banks, faculty of the Department of Anthropology, State University of New York (SUNY), Sister Toni Hajdaj, Sister Umm Aisha, Dr. AbdulAhad, Br. Ali Rifat and His wife Sister Yildiz at-Turki, Sheikh Dr. Omar of Maryland al-Hindi, Sheikh Tamer of Buffalo, and Sheikh Ali of Hartford Seminary, Sisters Asya Hamad, Amina Osman, and Fatima Samrodia of Darul-Ulum Madania of Buffalo for all their editing, suggestions and comments.

I want to also thank the team of Medina House Publishing in all their preparations and efforts at all stages of this book especially Br. Murat, Br. Khalid (Halit), Br. Mehmet (Matt), Br. Ahmed, and Sister Karen.

Lastly, I would like to thank all of my family members for their patience with me during the preparation of this book.

We ask Allah ﷻ to accept all our efforts with the Divine Karam, Fadl, and Grace but not with our faulty and limited efforts deeming rejection. اللَّهُمَّ صلِّ عَلى سَيِّدِناَ وَ حَبِيْبَنَا وَ مَوْلَانَا مُحَمَّد.

INDEX